The Parts That Had to Hide

The Parts That Had to Hide

An autistic perspective on survival, adaptation and living more authentically

by

Laura McGarrick

Pesky Publishing Ltd

First edition, 2026

ISBN 978-1-0687533-3-6

Published by Pesky Publishing Ltd

Author's Note

This is the book I wish I could have read years ago.

A book that reflected my own experiences, helped me see myself with greater compassion, and reminded me that I was not alone in the challenges I faced.

For much of my life, I struggled to understand why I found certain things so difficult when they seemed to come naturally to other people. I spent years analysing myself, trying harder, adapting more, and searching for explanations for why life often felt more challenging than it appeared to be for those around me.

Receiving an autism diagnosis helped me make sense of many of those experiences. It gave me a framework for understanding myself with greater clarity and compassion and allowed me to let go of some of the shame I had carried for years. Rather than seeing my difficulties as personal failings, I began to understand them as the result of living in a world that was not always designed with autistic people in mind.

At the same time, the diagnosis raised new questions. What happens when you have spent decades learning to hide parts of yourself? How do you begin to trust yourself after years of adapting to meet the expectations of others? And how do you separate who you are from the survival strategies you developed along the way?

This book grew out of those questions.

It is not intended to speak for every autistic person, as autism is diverse and deeply individual. Instead, it offers one autistic perspective on survival, adaptation, self understanding, and the gradual process of living more authentically.

Most of all, I hope that autistic readers, particularly those diagnosed later in life, find comfort in knowing that they are not alone.

Contents

Chapter One: The Parts That Had to Hide

The ways of adapting to survive described in this chapter do not emerge from failure or flaw on the part of the individual, but from what is required to stay safe as an autistic child in environments with people who do not recognise or respond to autistic needs. They form early, before there is language to describe what is happening, and before any real choice is possible.

At the time, these experiences are all that is known and allow connections with others to continue, reduce the likelihood of conflict and create the only form of stability available within environments that feel unpredictable and unsafe. The cost is usually not visible until much later into adulthood, often when they begin to break down and can no longer be sustained in the same way.

Learning to Take Up Less Space

Some autistic children come to suppress their natural way of being because it becomes clear, through repeated experience and often in subtle ways, that existing as they are is not fully accepted. Even without overt criticism, moments of confusion, correction, exclusion, or quiet disapproval begin to accumulate, shaping an understanding that it is safer to adjust than to be as they are.

This tends to show up in small, everyday ways: a sensitivity that is dismissed rather than acknowledged, a need that is overlooked because it is not expressed loudly, or a moment of distress that passes without response. In these contexts, where caregiving may be limited, inconsistent, or absorbed elsewhere, safety can come to depend on becoming less visible and needing less, asking for less, and expressing less so as not to draw attention to differences that are never met anyway.

This shift does not happen as a conscious decision, but as a gradual adaptation and the child begins to prioritise fitting in, avoiding negative reactions, or maintaining connection. Eventually, these adjustments accumulate until they no longer feel like adjustments at all, but simply the way life is supposed to be lived.

What Becomes Unspoken

As this pattern continues and the child grows, the full, authentic experience of the self begins to narrow and what is expressed becomes increasingly limited, often in ways so subtle they are not recognised at the time. Needs, sensitivities, and distress do not disappear, but are managed internally, with little expectation of being met with the care required.

This suppression often shows up as masking or camouflaging and the child may closely observe others and copy social behaviours, rehearse what to say, or force eye contact despite discomfort. They might hide stimming behaviours, push themselves through sensory overwhelm without outward reaction, or suppress responses that would otherwise communicate confusion or distress. In some cases, they appear mature for their age, becoming highly self-monitoring and carefully managing how they come across whereas others withdraw more quietly, becoming watchful, hesitant, and less outwardly expressive.

Emotional experience becomes more contained, more private, and increasingly handled alone and while this often makes the child appear well-adjusted on the surface, it is typically effortful. This may lead to fatigue, anxiety, emotional shutdown, or difficulty identifying their own needs, alongside a growing sense of disconnection from themselves.

What remains visible to others are the more socially acceptable parts: the parts that cope, comply, remain steady, and do not ask for much, or at least not in ways that would require a different response. What appears as adaptation is often a form of self-protection in environments where being authentic has not consistently felt safe or understood.

When Holding Everything Together Becomes Exhausting

Maintaining a socially acceptable version of the self carries an increasing internal cost.

Outwardly, things may appear steady although the strain is often held privately, without language for what is happening or any clear way of making sense of it. There can be ongoing effort involved in monitoring behaviour, adjusting responses and containing reactions that feel out of place in the current environment. For autistic people, this often includes managing sensory input, navigating social expectations that are not explicit, and suppressing signs of overload to remain acceptable within a given context.

Fatigue, physical symptoms, and emotional pressure may be present, but they are not always understood as signs of overload or unmet need. Instead, there can be a more general sense of being different, alongside the expectation to continue regardless, because there does not appear to be another viable option.

Because distress is internalised, it often remains unseen and the absence of visible struggle is taken as evidence of coping, rather than evidence of how much is being contained.

For autistic girls, this pattern is particularly intensified by gendered expectations as they are often expected to be accommodating, emotionally aware, and easy to manage. Distress may be tolerated when it is quiet and contained, while visible anger or resistance is discouraged, sometimes subtly, sometimes more directly. This may often lead to a form of survival that appears as maturity or resilience from the outside, while masking a significant and ongoing internal strain.

These early adaptations do not disappear with age but tend to follow into adulthood, shaping careers, relationships, and roles that reward reliability, endurance, and emotional containment. Continuing to function is often taken as evidence of strength, even as the physical body becomes increasingly unwell and mental health is affected. Sadly, with societal expectations so high, these periods of exhaustion or illness are more likely to be interpreted as personal failure than as the predictable outcome of prolonged, unsupported strain, which can make the experience even harder to understand.

When Survival Becomes Identity

When this way of functioning is established early and reinforced, it can begin to feel like personality rather than adaptation. Patterns such as being low-need, reliable, and emotionally contained may come to feel like inherent traits, rather than responses shaped by the need to remain safe and connected in dynamics that did not allow for adjustment.

Because these coping behaviours are used consistently and are rarely questioned, they do not feel like something the person is doing, but simply who they are. There is often no clear point of contrast, particularly when these adaptations formed before there was language for inner experience or any real possibility of choice. What developed in response to others is therefore taken as evidence of character, something fixed and intrinsic, rather than something that was necessary within a particular environment.

As a result, it can become difficult to distinguish between what reflects authentic autistic preference and what has been shaped by external pressure and adaptation. The absence of visible distress is taken as ease, and endurance is mistaken for strength, even when both are misleading. What appears steady on the surface may in fact reflect a sustained effort to contain, adjust, and remain acceptable within expectations that were never designed with the individual in mind. You may question how much of your personality has been a byproduct of having to survive chaos and how many of your choices were not really yours at all, but coping mechanisms disguised as decisions.

The Quiet Breaking Point

Eventually, this way of living begins to place demands on the body and mind that are difficult to sustain. Maintaining a socially acceptable version of the self requires ongoing monitoring including tracking one's behaviour, adjusting responses, anticipating reactions, and containing internal experience so that it does not become visible. This level of self-regulation draws heavily on cognitive and emotional resources, often without conscious awareness of the effort involved and why you are doing it.

Energy may deplete more quickly, and everyday demands begin to feel increasingly difficult to sustain, even if they once felt manageable. This shift does not always present dramatically but may appear as recurring illness, cognitive fatigue, increased sensitivity, or a growing sense that ordinary expectations are no longer tolerable in the same way. Because attention has been directed outward for so long, towards what is expected, appropriate, or safe, there may also be a gradual disconnection from internal cues such as need, preference, or early signs of overwhelm.

In the body, this sustained effort often reflects a prolonged stress response and even in the absence of immediate threat, tension may be held, sleep disrupted, digestion affected, and a sense of being unable to fully settle may persist. For some, this shifts towards shutdown, where energy is conserved and responsiveness reduced and, in both cases, the system is adapting to ongoing demand rather than operating from a place of ease.

Tasks that were once routine begin to require more effort than expected, and rest no longer restores in the way it used to, which can be as confusing as it is exhausting. Because this pattern has been normalised for so long, these changes are often misattributed to ageing, weight, personality, or supposed weakness and the response is often to push harder, rather than to pause, even when pushing no longer works.

For the autistic person, this tends to deepen frustration and confusion, particularly when others continue to reference earlier functioning as evidence of capability. What is often overlooked is that earlier functioning was frequently sustained through prolonged masking, endurance, and disconnection from internal limits, rather than through genuine capacity.

When the Pattern Becomes Visible

There may be moments of sudden clarity, where insight lands heavily, brings grief, disbelief, or a sense of disorientation and when you finally see it, when you feel it fully, it is not pretty but it is necessary. Alongside these are slower realisations, where understanding builds and begins to reshape how earlier experiences are seen, it feels heavy because it is the first time your internal reaction matches the reality of your experience.

Often, this recognition emerges at a point where continuing in the same way no longer feels possible with strategies that once held everything together begin to feel effortful rather than automatic, and exhaustion makes visible what was previously sustained without question. Tasks that were manageable may now feel disproportionate, and there can be a growing sense that something underlying has been missed or misunderstood, and you begin to ask yourself what is wrong.

What becomes visible is not only the pattern itself, but the conditions in which it developed, that can be difficult to fully take in at first and experiences that were previously minimised begin to be reinterpreted. There is recognition of how much was tolerated, how often distress was unsupported, and how frequently needs were overlooked, sometimes repeatedly. What was once understood as personal difficulty begins to be seen in a different light, as the consequence of prolonged lack of attunement, support, or protection. There is a rage that has always lived beneath the survival that builds further when you begin to realise how much of your life was shaped by someone else's dysfunction.

Patterns that once felt like part of the personality or seen as strengths begin to be recognised as adaptations. The effort involved becomes clearer, and what once felt like "this is just how I am" may begin to shift towards an understanding of "this is what I learned to do." And so, attention turns inward as well as outward, towards both internal experience and the systems and relationships that relied, whether consciously or not, on compliance, reliability, or emotional containment.

This may be particularly painful when it involves recognising that those closest may also have benefited from the pattern remaining intact, even if that was never explicitly acknowledged. There may be grief for what was not recognised earlier, alongside a growing awareness of needs that had little space to exist.

These realisations do not resolve the pattern, but they make it increasingly difficult to continue without question. As the previous way of functioning becomes harder to sustain, there is often a gradual movement towards something different, shaped less by endurance and more by the possibility of responding to one's own internal experience.

A Different Starting Point

Recognising these patterns does not undo what has been lived, nor does it immediately change how life is experienced. If anything, it can make things feel more unsettled for a time, particularly as familiar ways of functioning no longer feel workable, but alternatives are not yet fully clear. What once provided stability, even at a cost, begins to loosen, and there may be uncertainty about what remains when those patterns are no longer carried out in the same way.

As suppression and masking begin to ease, responses that were previously contained may become more noticeable. Sensory sensitivities may feel more intense, not because they have increased, but because they are no longer being pushed aside and emotional responses may become clearer or more immediate. There may also be a growing awareness of the discomfort, fatigue, or misalignment in situations that were previously endured without so much focus on how it truly felt.

This can create a period of instability within which the strategies that once maintained consistency are no longer used in the same way, but alternative ways of responding may not yet feel established. Decisions may begin to shift, what is tolerated, what is agreed to, and where energy is directed, but these changes can be difficult to navigate, both internally and within existing relationships or existing expectations.

Externally, this shift may not always be understood, and others may experience it as withdrawal, inconsistency, or difficulty; particularly if they were accustomed to a version of the person that was highly accommodating or contained. Internally, there may be doubt about whether these changes are valid, or whether something is being lost rather than regained.

What it does offer is a different starting point and the question is no longer how to continue enduring, but what becomes possible when the autistic experience is taken seriously, and when life is no longer organised around suppressing it.

Chapter Two: Growing Up Without a Mirror

Conditions, Not Essence

What shaped the pattern described in the previous chapter was not anything inherent to the autistic child, but the conditions they grew up within. Needs were present, distress existed and sensitivity was part of who the child was, but what was missing was attunement to the fact that these experiences required care, protection, or adjustment from the adults around them.

For an autistic child, this kind of attunement is not an additional layer of support, it's part of what makes their environment feel safe and navigable and when it is absent, that absence becomes part of the child's environment itself. A lack of response can come to feel ordinary rather than notable, and the absence of being met may not register as something missing, but as simply how things are. And so, the child adapts not only to what is present, but to what is not, organising themselves around an environment where needs are not expected to be met.

When Needs Are Present but Unmet

This book reflects the perspective of a late-diagnosed autistic adult, looking back on experiences that were lived without recognition or explanation at the time, and only later understood through diagnosis and new awareness.

For many, these patterns formed in a context where awareness of autism was limited, particularly for children who were quiet, compliant, or internally focused. While this context helps explain the lack of recognition, it does not remove the fact that the child's needs were present, whether they were responded to or not.

When needs are present but not met, the body continues to register them, but without consistent recognition or response, there is little framework for understanding what is being felt or what to do with it. Experiences such as sensitivity, discomfort, or overwhelm may be present, but without language or response, they are often managed internally, reduced in visibility, or adapted around.

For some autistic children, this is further shaped by alexithymia, or differences in emotional awareness, particularly in environments where emotional language is not offered or mirrored. Without repeated experiences of having internal states recognised and named, it can become more difficult to identify or differentiate what is being felt and sensations may be experienced more as general distress rather than clearly defined emotions.

In this context, signals that might otherwise prompt support are less likely to be recognised as such and needs remain present, but without a clear way of being understood, expressed, or responded to.

Distress Without Display

Autistic distress does not always show itself in ways that are easily recognised by others, particularly by neurotypical people.

For many autistic children, it is ongoing rather than episodic, and internal rather than outwardly expressed. There may be no obvious build-up, escalation, or behaviour that signals urgency, concern, or intervention and instead, distress is often contained, taking the form of quiet withdrawal, what appears as shyness, or a heightened level of internal effort to remain composed externally. This may include tolerating sensory discomfort without outward reaction, masking confusion in social situations, or suppressing the urge to withdraw in environments that feel overwhelming.

Because these responses do not draw attention, they are often misinterpreted as personality or temperament and a child may appear calm, compliant, or well-adjusted while experiencing significant internal strain. Increased fatigue, reduced tolerance, or a need for more time alone may be present but not recognised as signs of distress.

Autistic children may gravitate towards adults rather than peers in social situations, not because they are shy, but because interactions with other children can feel more unpredictable, fast-moving, and difficult to navigate. Peer dynamics often rely on subtle social cues, shifting rules, and unspoken expectations, which can leave an autistic child feeling unsure, exposed, or overwhelmed. Adults, by contrast, tend to communicate more directly, and may therefore feel more predictable and easier to engage with.

As a result, the child may withdraw from peer groups and remain close to adults as a way of regulating themselves and reducing social vulnerability. This is easily misread as shyness or a preference for solitude, when it may instead reflect an adaptive response to environments that feel confusing or socially risky.

Because distress remains contained and non-disruptive, it often goes largely unnoticed and what is lived internally as ongoing strain does not register externally as something that requires attention.

Adaptation Without Choice

Crying, withdrawal, or small acts of resistance may pass without response, and the message absorbed is that expressing need does not bring the right care and when an undiagnosed autistic child begins to realise, in whatever way they can, that their needs are not going to be understood or met, there is often a gradual shift from seeking support to adapting for survival.

Rather than continuing to express confusion, discomfort, or overwhelm and not being met with recognition, the child may start to suppress those signals and rely more heavily on coping strategies such as withdrawal, compliance, masking, or heightened self-monitoring. This can give rise to an internalised sense that their needs are "too much," misplaced, or unlikely to be responded to.

Often, a form of early self-reliance often develops, and the child begins to manage alone, not because independence is freely chosen, but because support is no longer expected to be available. What may appear as maturity or capability is frequently an adaptation shaped by necessity, where help-seeking reduces and self-regulation increases beyond what would ordinarily be developmentally appropriate.

The outward presentation may become quieter or more manageable, but internally this often comes at a cost, including increased anxiety, exhaustion, and a growing disconnection from their own cues and preferences. Needs do not disappear, but may be minimised, delayed, or experienced as secondary to maintaining stability and rather than an absence of need, what emerges is an adaptation to environments that feel consistently misattuned.

The pattern that develops does not arise from intention or personality but forms in environments where adults interpret behaviour, set expectations, and determine what is attended to and what is passed over.

Hypervigilance to Others

In the absence of consistent response, the child may become increasingly attuned to their environment to anticipate what is required of them and rather than relying on others for guidance or support, attention shifts outward, towards monitoring tone, mood, and subtle changes in behaviour. This heightened awareness is not simply perceptiveness, but a form of vigilance shaped by the need to navigate situations where expectations are not clearly communicated and support is not reliably available.

Hypervigilance in autistic children often develops as an adaptive response to environments that feel unpredictable, overwhelming, or misattuned to their needs. When a child repeatedly experiences confusion, correction, or emotional intensity without clear understanding, they may begin to closely monitor their surroundings to anticipate what will happen next and reduce the risk of getting it "wrong." This may lead to a heightened sensitivity to tone of voice, facial expression, body language, and even very subtle shifts in mood or atmosphere.

Through ongoing experience, the child may become unusually attuned to small changes that others might not consciously notice, such as a slight tension in someone's voice, a pause before a response, or a shift in energy in the room. This is not intuition in a vague sense, but a learned, pattern-based vigilance shaped by experience and the focus is not connection in the typical social sense, but prediction and self-protection: what is about to happen, and how should I respond?

While this may sometimes appear as perceptiveness or emotional awareness, it is often underpinned by a constant scanning for potential threat or misalignment and the child may adjust quickly in response, becoming quieter, more agreeable, or withdrawing altogether to maintain stability. Internally, however, this level of monitoring can be exhausting and may contribute to anxiety, difficulty relaxing, and a reduced sense of safety even in neutral environments.

Therefore, hypervigilance is less about heightened social ease and more about heightened social risk management, a strategy that develops when understanding and safety are not reliably provided from the outside.

Autonomy Constrained

These dynamics are often reinforced beyond the caregiving environment.

Educational settings and wider systems tend to respond to children whose distress is outwardly expressed, while those who remain quiet and compliant are left largely unseen. The child who internalises distress is therefore less likely to receive support and more likely to be assumed to be coping and in these environments, expectations may be rigid and autonomy limited, leaving little room for the child to adjust their surroundings or respond in ways that align with their needs.

Instead, they are required to adapt to externally imposed structures, often without flexibility or understanding. This reinforces a pattern in which monitoring, compliance, and internal management become necessary, particularly in environments where difference is less tolerated and support is not attuned to the child's experience.

What develops under these conditions is not selflessness, but adaptation in which autonomy is gradually overridden. Basic care may still be present, meals arrive, clothes are clean and the household functions, yet, the environment may remain loud, tense, unpredictable, or emotionally unsafe and the child has little protection from conflict, intrusion, or sensory overwhelm, and no reliable place for distress to go.

Perceived Strength Without Support

These experiences may create a lasting ambiguity in later life, where difficulty exists without a clear explanation. Because the child was fed and clothed, there may be an assumption, from others and sometimes internally, that they were cared for "well enough." Yet autistic safety is not only about provision, but also about steadiness, protection, and being treated with gentleness when the world is overwhelming.

When that layer is missing, survival can appear functional while remaining internally exhausting and a difficult contradiction develops. The person is experienced by others as capable, calm, and reliable; the one who manages, organises, explains, and holds things together and this presentation is often taken as strength or maturity, particularly in autistic girls.

As a result, roles may form in which the individual gives, supports, and stabilises others, while receiving little in return as support flows outward but is rarely directed back. This is not simply a pattern of behaviour, but a continuation of earlier conditions and needs remain unrecognised, both externally and internally, and the expectation of being met remains low.

Sensitivity Is Not a Deficit

Autistic sensitivity is not a weakness or a deficit- it reflects a nervous system that takes in more information, more quickly, and with less filtering.

Sensory input, emotional atmospheres, relational shifts, and environmental unpredictability may all be registered with greater intensity and what determines the impact of this sensitivity is not its presence, but whether it is met with care, understanding, and adjustment.

In environments where this sensitivity is recognised, it can support awareness, perception, and responsiveness. However, in environments where it is dismissed, minimised, or misunderstood, it becomes a source of strain.

What is often interpreted as "too much" is, in reality, too much for the environment to accommodate, rather than too much for the person to experience and when this distinction is not made, the individual may come to carry the responsibility for what is, in part, a mismatch between sensitivity and environment.

Overwhelming Environments

For many autistic people, sensitivity exists within environments that offer little protection from overwhelm. Noise remains constant, expectations are ongoing and often unclear, and the nervous system continues to register everything, while the environment remains unchanged.

In these conditions, the burden of adjustment falls on the individual and rather than the environment being adapted, the person is expected to tolerate, filter, and manage internally. Sensitivity does not lessen, but is contained, redirected, or worked around and the result is not resolution, but continued exposure without relief.

A pattern begins to form in which increasing amounts are managed internally, while external demands remain the same. Effort increases, but recognition does not and over time, this creates a growing imbalance between what is experienced and what is acknowledged and the nervous system remains exposed, while the capacity to continue in the same way gradually reduces.

What follows is not sudden, but cumulative.

Adapting Without Accommodation

Because environments are rarely well suited to the autistic individual, nor adjusted appropriately, the responsibility for adaptation falls almost entirely on the individual. Noise-cancelling headphones, routines, controlled exposure, and carefully managed environments are not preferences but ways of reducing internal strain.

These adaptations can allow access where none would otherwise be possible. Yet even with them in place, access often remains limited as certain environments may still be too overwhelming, too unpredictable, or too demanding to enter or remain within and participation becomes conditional, dependent on how much can be managed, reduced, or endured.

Where environments are adapted, even slightly, the impact can be immediate and situations that were previously overwhelming may become tolerable enough to engage with, not because sensitivity has changed, but because the conditions have.

In the absence of such adjustment, adaptation becomes ongoing. The individual continues to modify, manage, and work around environments that remain unchanged and leads to a gradual narrowing of where they can go, what they can take part in, and how they move through the world.

The cost is not only practical, but cumulative and effort is continually directed towards making environments bearable, rather than towards engagement, exploration, or rest.

Masking as Necessity

What is often described as coping is, in many cases, sustained effort and masking becomes less a choice and more a necessity within environments that do not adjust. The nervous system remains alert, monitoring, adjusting, and suppressing responses that might lead to negative consequences or misunderstanding.

This may involve controlling facial expression, managing tone, rehearsing responses, forcing eye contact, or suppressing movements and reactions that would otherwise communicate discomfort or overwhelm and what appears calm from the outside often reflects containment rather than ease.

The effort involved is ongoing with attention directed not only towards the environment, but towards the self, monitoring what is said, how it is said, how it might be received, and what needs to be changed to remain acceptable within the situation.

Masking does not reduce demand; it redistributes it internally and because this pattern develops early, it may not be recognised as effort and it can feel like the only available way of being, rather than an adaptation shaped by context.

While masking may reduce immediate risk or discomfort in social situations, it does not remove the underlying strain. Instead, it shifts it inward and energy is used to maintain presentation, rather than to support regulation or recovery.

As a result, what is sustained outwardly as composure often corresponds internally to increased pressure and the absence of visible distress is taken as evidence of coping, even as the effort required to maintain it continues to accumulate.

Inner Experience, Outer Expression

For many autistic people, a gap develops between what is experienced internally and what is visible externally and a mismatch may begin to form, where what is felt is not what is shown.

Outward expression tends to align with what is socially acceptable, rather than with the full reality of what is being felt. This is not because the internal experience is unclear or insignificant, but because it has not been met with recognition or response in ways that allow it to be expressed safely.

As masking becomes more established, what is presented outwardly reflects what is expected, manageable, or permitted within the environment. What is lived internally may remain unspoken, unshared, or gradually set aside, not through absence, but through lack of response.

Inner experience becomes increasingly private, not because it lacks significance, but because it has not been met with response and what develops is not a reduction in feeling, but a separation between experience and expression.

This creates a sense of distance from one's own internal state, where what is known internally does not fully translate into what is expressed or recognised externally.

Relational Perception

This sensitivity also extends beyond sensory experience and many autistic people notice relational patterns with clarity; inconsistencies, emotional undercurrents, power dynamics, and misalignment between what is said and what is done. Repeated dynamics may be recognised across people's lives and within their relationships, often with a sense of where these patterns originate.

This is not vague intuition, but pattern-based perception shaped through experience with subtle invalidations, shifts in tone, and relational tensions that others may not consciously register becoming visible.

In environments shaped by performance or unspoken rules, this perceptiveness can be uncomfortable for others. Rather than being valued, it may be minimised, reframed, or dismissed, not because it is inaccurate, but because it draws attention to things others may prefer not to examine.

As a result, the individual may begin to question their own perception, particularly when it is repeatedly met with dismissal or contradiction and what is seen clearly is not always acknowledged externally.

This ability can become intertwined with earlier adaptations, and the individual may find themselves anticipating, interpreting, or making sense of others to navigate relationships more safely. There can be a subtle pull towards becoming the one who understands, explains, or holds what is unspoken, yet this role carries a cost, placing the individual in a position of managing dynamics that are not theirs to carry.

Relational pattern perception can be used for orientation rather than responsibility. It can support recognising where something does not feel safe, aligned, or sustainable, without requiring interpretation, explanation, or correction of others.

However, the individual is not and was never required to be the translator of other people's inner worlds, nor the holder of experiences that were never theirs to resolve.

What this perception offers is not a demand to engage more deeply, but the ability to choose differently. To recognise patterns earlier, to leave situations that do not align, and to move towards environments that do not require constant interpretation.

For some, this may come at the cost of belonging within certain spaces, allowing for a different kind of alignment, one that does not depend on self-betrayal.

Endurance, Not Ease

Sensitivity that is left unsupported does not disappear with age and instead becomes woven into how life is lived.

What is often described from the outside as strength or independence is more accurately a history of endurance and for many autistic adults, recognition does not come through care from others, but through the point at which continuation is no longer possible.

What changes is not that the world becomes easier, but that sensitivity can no longer be carried without consequence.

Chapter Three: The Shadow of Anger

Why Anger Is Met with Fear

Anger is one of the emotions most likely to be treated as unacceptable in many social contexts and is often framed as something that needs to be controlled, softened, or removed altogether, rather than understood as a meaningful response to experience.

For autistic people, anger is rarely recognised as an emotional signal and more often, it is interpreted as a behavioural problem. Distress may be read as hostility, refusal as defiance, and boundary-setting as rudeness and in these contexts, anger is not approached with curiosity or care but met with fear and attempts to suppress it.

What is being expressed is not recognised for what it is and rather than looking at what has led to this point, the focus shifts to stopping the expression itself. The conditions in which anger arises, overwhelm, confusion, misattunement, or accumulated strain, are easily overlooked.

From early on, many autistic people learn that anger does not lead to support or protection. Instead, it brings escalation, punishment, or withdrawal of care and therefore anger becomes associated not with safety, but with risk.

As a result, anger is not only misunderstood, but increasingly withheld.

Overload, Not Aggression

Autistic anger is often misunderstood because it is interpreted through frameworks that prioritise behavioural control over meaning.

What appears to be a sudden reaction is often the endpoint of cumulative overload with sensory input, ongoing pressure, and unprocessed stress accumulating gradually, while early signs go unrecognised or are not responded to. Therefore, the internal build-up remains largely invisible.

By the time a response becomes visible, the threshold has already been exceeded, and this is not an escalation from calm to anger, but a progression from unrecognised strain to overload.

For those who experience alexithymia, recognising and articulating emotional states can be difficult- internal changes may not be clearly identified as they develop, limiting the ability to signal the need for space, rest, or relief before that threshold is reached.

What appears exaggerated from the outside by others is often the result of a long, contained internal process and what is expressed in a moment may reflect what has been carried for far longer.

Meltdown as Response

In these moments, behaviour is not an attempt to control others but an involuntary nervous system response.

What is often labelled as aggression is more accurately understood as a meltdown; a response to overwhelming emotional or sensory input. Meltdowns are not tantrums, defiance, or manipulation and they indicate that the limit of what can be managed has been reached.

What appears outwardly as anger is often the point at which accumulated strain can no longer be contained and the intensity of the response reflects what has been building, not simply what is happening in the present moment.

Sometimes, this overwhelm moves outward as a meltdown and at others, it moves inward as a shutdown. In a shutdown, expression reduces rather than intensifies and there may be withdrawal, silence, dissociation, or an inability to respond. While less visible, the level of overwhelm is not reduced; it is contained differently.

Both are responses to the same underlying condition: distress that has not been recognised, supported, or met.

When these responses are treated as behavioural problems, the meaning of anger is lost and the focus shifts from understanding what led to the response, to stopping it as quickly as possible.

Anger and Gender Expectations

Expectations around anger are not applied equally and from early on, many girls are encouraged to be accommodating, polite, and emotionally attuned to others. Being "good," "nice," or easy to manage is reinforced, while expressions of anger are discouraged, corrected, or made uncomfortable to show.

For autistic girls, this often intensifies an existing pattern of internalisation where distress may already go unnoticed, anger is not only unrecognised but shaped into something more acceptable.

Direct expression is reduced in favour of compliance, self-containment, or quiet endurance and the anger itself does not disappear but becomes less visible. Rather than being expressed openly, it may emerge indirectly through withdrawal, self-criticism, relational tension, or forms of aggression that are less likely to be recognised as such.

Because this does not match familiar ideas of anger, it is often overlooked or misread and the signal remains, but the form it takes changes.

This shapes how relationships are navigated and attention turns outward, towards maintaining harmony, anticipating others' needs, and avoiding disruption and boundaries may become less defined, not through absence of need, but through repeated experience that expressing them does not lead to being met.

What develops is often described as kindness, reliability, or emotional maturity and what is less visible is the role that suppressed anger has played in shaping that pattern. Therefore, anger is not absent, but it is contained, redirected, or absorbed.

Splitting Anger Off

When an emotion repeatedly leads to negative consequences, it becomes something to manage at a distance and something to control, or even fear and some people come to experience anger as a separate part of themselves. Over time, the message is absorbed: this part of me is not safe to express. Rather than disappearing, anger is redirected and it is softened, hidden, or replaced with more acceptable responses such as compliance, politeness, or withdrawal and what develops may be described as maturity, kindness, or emotional control, while the role of suppressed anger remains largely unseen.

This is not avoidance or immaturity but an adaptive response to an emotion that has not been allowed safe expression.

What Happens When Anger Has Nowhere to Go

Anger does not disappear when it is suppressed. It changes direction and instead of being expressed outwardly, it often turns inward, becoming self-criticism, exhaustion, or shutdown and can contribute to burnout, emotional numbness, depression, and a persistent sense of vigilance.

For many, particularly autistic girls, anger becomes associated with risk to connection. Being "good," quiet, and easy to manage is often what is met with acceptance and anger, by contrast, risks rejection, correction, or withdrawal of care.

As a result, anger is not only contained but internalised and it may take the form of shame, a sense of being "too much," or a belief that one's needs are unreasonable or unsafe to express.

The cost is not always immediate, but it accumulates quietly and what is lost is not only the expression of anger, but the information it carries about limits and boundaries.

Anger as Information

Anger is not random and it often arises at the point where a boundary has been crossed, autonomy has been undermined, or something is happening without consent and in this sense, anger is not excess emotion, but information.

Rather than asking how to eliminate anger, it can be more useful to ask what it is responding to.

What is being violated.
What is being ignored.
What has gone unrecognised for too long.

When it is listened to, anger brings clarity, it identifies limits and signals where something is not right, not fair, or not sustainable- it is part of how the nervous system communicates that something requires attention or change.

When anger is consistently treated as a problem, this meaning is lost. The focus shifts to controlling the response rather than understanding what led to it and this creates a disconnection not only from anger, but from the information it carries.

Righteous Anger

Not all anger is reactive or overwhelming, some anger is proportionate, reflecting a clear response to injustice, harm, or misuse of power and it protects dignity and signals that something is not acceptable.

For many autistic people, particularly those who have been expected to be accommodating or "easier," this kind of anger is often suppressed early and the pressure to remain calm, polite, or compliant can override the instinct to resist or object. When this happens, the situation anger responds to does not disappear but absorbed and this can create confusion about where responsibility lies, whether harm is real, and whether one is allowed to name it.

The absence of outwardly expressed anger is not always a sign of peace and may reflect a history of learning that recognising and responding to what is wrong carries a cost and so listening to anger does not mean acting without reflection but recognising it as a signal rather than dismissing it as a fault.

What changes is not the presence of anger, but the relationship to it and when that relationship shifts, what was once suppressed begins to return as clarity, as direction, and as the capacity to say: this is not acceptable.

Why Anger Comes to Feels Unacceptable

Anger often comes to feel unacceptable not because it is inherently harmful, but because of the consequences attached to expressing it - when anger is met with fear, correction, dismissal, or punishment, the message is learned quickly: this is not safe to express.

For many autistic children, this happens repeatedly with distress already misunderstood, and when anger emerges as part of that distress, it is often interpreted as behaviour to be managed rather than communication to be understood.

The response that follows shapes what happens next and if anger leads to withdrawal of care, loss of connection, criticism, or being seen as "difficult," the cost of expressing it becomes clear and the child adapts. This is reinforced by wider expectations because being calm, agreeable, and easy to manage is often rewarded. Being angry is not and, for girls, there is often an added pressure to be polite, accommodating, and emotionally controlled.

What develops is not an absence of anger, but a learned relationship to it where it is held back, softened, redirected, or internalised. The sense that anger is unacceptable is not inherent but shaped through experience, through what happens when it is shown, and through what is at stake if it is expressed again.

Allowing Anger to Exist

Allowing anger to exist does not mean acting on it but recognising it, naming it, and acknowledging it as meaningful. It can be held internally without needing to be expressed outwardly in every situation, it does not have to be suppressed to be contained, and it does not have to be acted on to be valid. For many, this may be the first experience of anger without consequence.

It can be recognised privately, even if it is not understood or accepted by others and can be acknowledged without being dismissed, minimised, or explained away and that acknowledgement matters because even when no one else recognises what is happening, recognising it oneself is a shift and it marks a move away from self-suppression towards alignment with one's own experience.

This creates the possibility of a different response and rather than being something to fear or avoid, anger can begin to be worked with, informing decisions, clarifying limits, and contributing to change.

What is important is not whether anger is expressed in every moment, but whether it is allowed to be exist.

When Anger Leads to Change

This is where change begins, as awareness of anger gradually brings awareness of limits, making it clearer what is and is not acceptable, what can continue, and what can no longer be sustained.

Relationships or roles that once relied on silence may begin to feel increasingly difficult to maintain, not because anything has suddenly changed externally, but because something internally is no longer willing to accommodate in the same way.

This kind of understanding rarely comes easily and often develops through difficult experience; through recognising what has been tolerated for too long, and what can no longer continue without cost. Boundaries are not always known in advance, but take shape through what has been crossed, through moments that make clear where a limit exists.

What begins to shift is not only how anger is understood, but how it is used, no longer something to suppress, but something that informs decisions, shapes relationships, and supports a more grounded sense of self-protection.

Anger as Part of the Self

Anger is not something to eliminate. It is part of the self that carries information about harm, autonomy, and dignity and reclaiming it is not an act of aggression, but an act of integration.

The relationship to it is therefore no longer something to suppress, but becomes something that can be recognised, understood, and used to inform decisions, shape relationships, and support a more grounded sense of self-protection.

For many late-diagnosed autistic adults, this process is less about becoming someone new, and more about allowing what has always been present to exist without suppression. This does not come without difficulty and often requires unlearning patterns of compliance, tolerating discomfort, and facing the reality of what has been endured, leading to further clarity.

Anger begins to function as it was always meant to; not as something overwhelming or dangerous, but as a signal that something matters, that something has been crossed, and that something is no longer acceptable.

Chapter Four: Sensitivity Without Recognition

Sensitivity Without Recognition

Sensitivity is an intrinsic part of the autistic experience, but the degree of strain it creates depends largely on the conditions in which it exists. It is not simply heightened reaction, but a nervous system that registers more; more detail, more intensity, more change.

Sensory input, emotional tone, relational shifts, and environmental unpredictability are often experienced with a depth that is not immediately visible from the outside and when this sensitivity is recognised, it can be supported, regulated, and integrated into daily life. When it is not, however, its impact does not disappear.; it is carried internally instead, often without acknowledgement or relief.

For many autistic people, sensitivity was never something that was met with curiosity or understanding. It was present, consistent, and often intense, yet received little meaningful response and what shapes the impact of this sensitivity is not its presence, but whether it is recognised and responded to.

Instead of being understood as information, it is often dismissed, minimised, or reframed as overreaction. Distress may be overlooked, discomfort may be normalised, and the need for adjustment may be treated as unnecessary.

When this happens repeatedly, the individual is left to manage experiences that exceed what the environment supports and the nervous system continues to register everything, while the environment remains unchanged.

This creates a particular kind of strain; not only from what is being experienced, but from the absence of recognition. What is felt internally does not match what is acknowledged externally and eventually, this mismatch begins to shape how experience is processed- sensitivity becomes something to manage privately, rather than something that is supported collectively.

What may appear from the outside as resilience or independence is often adaptation in the absence of understanding, with the difficulty experienced not being sensitivity itself, but existing in a society in which what is felt is not recognised.

Sensitivity as Responsiveness, Not Impairment

Autistic sensitivity reflects a nervous system that takes in more information, more quickly, and with less filtering, which means that experience is not reduced or softened in the same way, but remains present in its detail and intensity.

Sounds, light, movement, emotional atmospheres, relational shifts, and environmental unpredictability are often registered immediately and held, rather than fading into the background. Where others may unconsciously filter, prioritise, and discard, autistic perception tends to remain more open, allowing more to be noticed, more to be retained, and more to be processed at once.

This is not a deficit in processing, but a difference in how information is received and organised. The result is not simply "greater sensitivity," but a greater volume of input moving through the system at any given time, which can bring clarity and depth in supportive conditions, but strain when environments are fast, unpredictable, or unresponsive.

What determines the impact of this sensitivity is whether it is recognised and responded to. When it is met with care, protection, and adjustment, it can be integrated into daily life in a way that feels manageable and coherent. When it is dismissed or reframed as excessive, its impact does not lessen, but is instead carried internally, often without acknowledgement or relief.

This eventually creates a particular kind of imbalance in which the environment remains unchanged, while the individual absorbs the cost of adapting to it. What is often interpreted as overreaction is, in many cases, the natural consequence of a system that has taken in more than it can comfortably process, without the external conditions shifting to meet it.

When this way of processing is not recognised, the responsibility for managing it falls almost entirely on the individual, shaping not only how they respond to the world, but how they come to understand themselves within it.

Managing Ongoing Exposure

When sensitivity remains unsupported, the task becomes not only managing input but managing how that input is responded to and interpreted by others.

Masking develops within this space as a way of navigating both expectation and exposure at the same time and the nervous system stays alert, continually monitoring, anticipating, and adjusting responses to avoid negative consequences, while also trying to stay within tolerable limits internally.

What appears calm from the outside often reflects containment rather than ease, as responses are held back or reshaped rather than expressed freely and this state does not resolve on its own and tends to build quietly, particularly in the absence of recognition, recovery, or spaces where experience can be processed.

Life Without a Pause

When there is no consistent opportunity for the nervous system to settle, life does not necessarily fall apart in obvious ways. It can continue, outwardly intact, while internally becoming organised around staying alert.

There may be no single moment that marks something as wrong, no clear crisis to point to and instead, there is a steady sense of readiness, a quiet anticipation that something could happen at any moment, even in situations that appear calm from the outside. Rest does not fully land, stillness does not fully register and the body remains slightly braced, as though it is waiting for something it cannot quite name.

This way of existing can begin to feel normal because there has been no consistent experience of anything different and without contrast, it is difficult to recognise that the baseline itself is shaped by strain.

Where Distress Is Held

When sensitivity is repeatedly dismissed or overlooked, the impact does not disappear. It shifts and what is not recognised or responded to relationally is often carried internally instead, and the body becomes the place where that accumulation is finally felt.

Distress that has no clear outlet or acknowledgement does not remain abstract. It settles into lived experience, sometimes showing up as ongoing exhaustion, low energy, recurring illness, or states that resemble burnout or flu-like depletion, where the only relief comes through withdrawal and rest.

These patterns can feel confusing, especially when there is no obvious cause, yet they are not random. They reflect a nervous system that has been taking in more than it has been able to process, hold, or recover from, often for longer than is visible from the outside.

Burnout Without Language

For many late-diagnosed autistic adults, there was no framework for understanding what was happening within their nervous system and experiences of overwhelm, exhaustion, or shutdown were felt clearly, but not named in a way that made sense.

Instead, distress was interpreted through whatever language was available at the time: physical illness, anxiety, depression, or fatigue. While these descriptions can capture parts of the experience, they often miss what sits underneath them, which is a system under sustained strain rather than a series of separate problems.

Burnout rarely arrives as a single, recognisable event. More often, it develops through repeated cycles of depletion and partial recovery, where each episode is treated in isolation while the conditions that produce it remain unchanged. This creates a pattern that feels difficult to trace, because nothing appears to have a clear beginning or end.

Burden, Not Ease

When nothing fully breaks, yet nothing fully settles, a particular way of living can take shape. It can look like coping, even like resilience from the outside, while internally it is held together through effort that is rarely visible.

This is not ease, and it is not growth but the ability to keep going while carrying more than was ever meant to be carried alone, often without realising just how much has been taken on and, gradually, sensitivity, adaptation, and exhaustion stop feeling like separate things. They begin to merge into a single, lived experience shaped by environments that remain unchanged, where the responsibility for adjustment sits almost entirely with the individual.

Chapter Five: The Cost of Constant Adaptation

For many autistic people, adaptation begins early and continues throughout life. It is not always recognised as adaptation at the time and instead becomes woven into how life is lived, shaping responses, behaviour, and ways of relating without being named as effort.

Because it is continuous, it rarely draws attention to itself and there is no clear starting point or obvious moment where it can be said to have begun. It becomes part of the background of experience, something carried rather than questioned or reflected upon.

What may appear from the outside as coping, resilience, or independence from the outside often reflects sustained internal effort and there is ongoing monitoring, adjusting, and containing of responses to remain aligned with expectations that were not designed with autistic experience in mind.

This process is rarely visible, and it is not always understood, even by the person living it and what is taken for granted as functioning is often supported by a constant negotiation between what is needed internally, what is required externally, and it is within that gap that strain begins to build.

Living at a Distance from the Self

When adaptation is continuous, it can create a gradual distance from internal experience. Attention is placed outward, toward what is expected, what is required, and how to respond in ways that will be accepted or understood.

Internal signals may still be present, but they are often deprioritised or overridden to maintain functioning and this outward orientation becomes familiar. They are set aside, softened or overridden to maintain stability within the extremal environment, and what is felt is still there but not always what guides decisions and actions.

Parts of experience that are not easily expressed or received can begin to recede from awareness because they have not found a place where they can exist openly. And so, certain feelings, needs or responses become less accessible and held ata distance, rather than integrated into everyday life.

This does not mean the self is absent but remains present yet not always centred. The point of reference shifts outward, and a sense of disconnection can develop, not because of a lack of identity or individuality, but from a way of living that has required parts of that identity to be set aside.

The Accumulation of Strain

The impact of constant adaptation is rarely immediate. It develops gradually, often in ways that are difficult to trace back to a single cause and may only become noticeable when the effort required to maintain everyday life begins to shift.

Fatigue can become more persistent, and recovery may take longer, with rest not restoring what has been depleted. At the same time, tolerance for noise, demand, or social interaction may begin to narrow, not suddenly, but in a way that is felt through increased sensitivity to what was previously manageable.

There can be a growing sense that everyday life requires more effort than it once did, even if external expectations have not changed. Tasks that were once straightforward may begin to feel heavier, and engagement may require more deliberate energy than before.

Without a clear point of reference, this shift can be difficult to make sense of. The change is felt and acknowledged, but not easily explained, which can be confusing, particularly when there is no clear explanation for why things feel more demanding.

When Functioning Becomes Harder to Sustain

There often comes a point where the level of effort required to maintain previous patterns becomes difficult to sustain and what had been held together through constant adjustment begins to feel more fragile, as though it depends on a level of energy that is no longer consistently available.

Tasks that were once manageable may begin to feel overwhelming, because the capacity to absorb them has shifted and situations that were previously tolerated may now feel unworkable. The margin for flexibility narrows in ways that are difficult to predict or control.

This shift is not always gradual or predictable in its unfolding, and may appear as a sudden loss of capacity, as if something changed overnight, while in reality it reflects a longer process of accumulated strain that has reached its limit.

From the outside, it may be interpreted as a decline in functioning but from the inside, it reflects a limit that has been reached and can no longer be carried in the same way.

Burnout as a Lived Experience

Burnout is often described in terms of exhaustion, but it is more than that. It can involve cognitive fatigue, reduced tolerance for sensory input, difficulty with tasks that were once routine, and a general sense that the systems used to manage life are no longer holding in the same way.

This is not a temporary dip in energy, nor something that resolves with rest alone. Instead, it reflects a state that develops when sustained effort is not matched by adequate recovery or support, so that strain continues to build without being properly relieved.

Because there is no clear framework for understanding this experience, it may be interpreted through more familiar terms such as depression, anxiety, or chronic fatigue. While these can overlap, they do not always account for the underlying cause, particularly where prolonged adaptation, sensory overload, and unmet needs have been present for an extended period of time.

What is being experienced is not simply tiredness, but a nervous system that has been required to continue beyond what it can sustainably manage.

Misinterpretation and Self-Blame

Without a framework for understanding what is happening, these changes are often misinterpreted. They may be attributed to personal weakness, lack of motivation, or a failure to cope, particularly in environments that place value on consistency, productivity, and outward functioning.

In response, there may be attempts to push through, to restore previous levels of functioning, or to meet expectations that are no longer sustainable. Effort increases, often significantly, but without addressing the underlying strain, so that what is visible is continued effort, while what remains unrecognised is the cost of maintaining it.

What is not accounted for is that the difficulty arises from cumulative impact of prolonged adaptation and that the individual is not failing to cope; they are continuing under conditions that require more than can be sustainably managed.

When this distinction is not made, the explanation turns inward and experiences that reflect overload, exhaustion, or reduced capacity are interpreted as personal shortcomings rather than as responses to sustained demand. This can shape how those experiences are understood, so that what is being lived is filtered through a lens of self-blame rather than recognised as the result of ongoing, unacknowledged strain.

The Erosion of Self-Trust

Within this experience, self-trust can begin to erode. Internal signals may start to feel unreliable, particularly when they conflict with external expectations or past experience, and uncertainty can develop around what is manageable and what is not.

Rather than being recognised as valid information, these signals are often filtered through doubt. There may be a growing tendency to check internal responses against what is expected or considered acceptable, so that what is felt directly is no longer taken at face value, but questioned, adjusted, or overridden.

When limits are repeatedly exceeded in this way, it becomes increasingly difficult to recognise where they are. This does not mean the limits are not there, but that access to them has become inconsistent, shaped by repeated experiences in which they could not be acted on or were not supported.

This may lead to a more general sense of disconnection from internal experience with decisions feeling less clear, boundaries harder to define, and the link between what is felt and what is acted upon becomes less stable.

The Loss of Joy and Spontaneity

Constant adaptation can begin to affect the experience of joy in ways that are not always immediately obvious. When attention is focused on managing, monitoring, and maintaining, there is less space available for spontaneity or ease, and activities may gradually become organised around what is tolerable rather than what is genuinely enjoyable.

Energy is directed toward sustaining functioning, which can make it more difficult to access the sense of curiosity, play, or immersion that often underpins enjoyment. What once felt engaging may begin to feel effortful, not because interest has disappeared, but because the capacity to reach it is reduced under ongoing strain.

Spontaneity becomes increasingly constrained. Responses are more likely to be shaped by what is manageable, expected, or predictable, rather than by what feels natural in the moment, and this can create a subtle but growing distance from experiences that might otherwise feel meaningful.

Joy is not absent, it becomes less accessible, often dependent on conditions that allow the nervous system enough space to settle and, what changes is the ability to move freely enough to experience them.

When Adaptation Is No Longer Sustainable

There often comes a point at which continuing in the same way is no longer possible. This may be recognised gradually, through increasing difficulty and reduced capacity, or it may become clear more abruptly, as a noticeable shift in what can be managed.

What was once endured can no longer be maintained in the same way and attempts to return to previous levels of functioning may no longer succeed, regardless of effort.

This point is not always immediately understood. It can feel confusing, particularly when there has been a long history of pushing through or adapting successfully, making the change seem sudden rather than the result of something that has been building over time.

Rather than reflecting a personal failure, this shift indicates that the cost of sustained adaptation has reached a limit and what is being encountered is not a loss of ability, but a recognition of capacity.

Recognising the Cost

Understanding the cost of constant adaptation does not immediately change external circumstances. Environments do not chnage, the same relationship dynamics remain and the expectations within them may still be present but, what begins to change is how those experiences are understood.

The difficulty is no longer seen as random or as a reflection of personal inadequacy, but as the result of sustained effort in conditions that have required more than could be consistently given and what once felt confusing or self-defining starts to make sense within a wider context.

This recognition does not remove the strain, but it alters its meaning and instead of asking why things feel harder or why capacity seems to fluctuate, there is a growing awareness that the system has been under prolonged demand without sufficient support or adjustment.

Therefore, recognising the cost becomes less about identifying a problem to fix, and more about understanding what has been happening all along.

A Shift in Perspective

From this point, a different perspective begins to emerge and rather than continuing to focus on how to adapt more effectively, attention gradually turns toward what is sustainable and what is not.

Questions begin to shift in tone and direction. Instead of asking how to maintain previous levels of functioning, there is space to consider what reduces strain, what allows for regulation, and what it might mean to organise life in a way that does not depend on constant override.

These questions are not always easy to answer, and they do not lead to immediate change. But what they offer is a reorientation, a movement away from endurance as the default and toward a more considered relationship with capacity, limits, and need.

The shift is often subtle at first, but it marks an important change: the beginning of seeing internal experience not as something to work against, but as something to work with.

Chapter Six: Autonomy, Demand and Resistance

When Autonomy Is Not Recognised

For many autistic people, particularly those diagnosed later in life, autonomy is not something that was consistently recognised or supported in early environments. Preferences, limits, and internal states were often present from the beginning, yet they were not always treated as meaningful or reliable sources of information.

Instead, expectations were largely defined externally, with little adjustment for how those expectations were experienced and what felt manageable, overwhelming, or misaligned internally did not necessarily shape what was asked.

Over time this creates a quiet but persistent disconnect and the gap that forms is not a matter of willingness or effort. It reflects a difference between what is being required and what can be sustained, where internal capacity is repeatedly negotiated in order to meet external demand. In this context, autonomy is not absent, but it is often overridden, deprioritised, or gradually moved out of the centre of decision-making.

When Expectation Overrides Experience

In dynamics where compliance is prioritised, internal experience can begin to take a secondary place, with requests, demands, and expectations treated as reasonable by default, regardless of how they are received or processed. For the autistic person, this can create a constant tension between what is being asked and what can realistically be tolerated or sustained.

This tension is not always visible, as what appears outwardly as compliance can sit alongside internal strain, hesitation, or a growing sense of resistance that is not easily expressed.

Resistance as a Response

Resistance is often misunderstood and frequently framed as avoidance, oppositional behaviour, or a lack of cooperation, and in some cases described through labels such as pathological demand avoidance. These patterns are real, and for many children and adults they are significant and impactful. However, the language used to describe them does not always account for the conditions in which they take shape.

Resistance does not emerge in isolation, it develops in context when internal limits are repeatedly overridden, and when there is little room for negotiation, adjustment, or refusal. Resistance can begin to form as a way of maintaining some sense of control or autonomy and this is not always conscious, and it is not simply a deliberate choice. It can show up as hesitation, withdrawal, or difficulty engaging, even in situations that appear manageable from the outside.

Responding to demand can shift from something that is negotiated to something that is endured, and it is within this shift that resistance begins to make sense. What is often described as avoidance can reflect an accumulated experience of being required to meet expectations that do not align with internal capacity, where saying no has not felt available or has carried consequences.

Therefore, resistance is not best understood as a lack of willingness, but as a response shaped over time by the experience of limited autonomy. The behaviours that are observed are real, but they do not exist separately from the environments in which they developed.

Demand and the Nervous System

For many autistic people, demands are not experienced as neutral and even everyday requests can carry a sense of pressure that is felt physically, as the nervous system responds to the expectation itself rather than just the task being asked. This is not simply about the content of the demand, but the way it is received, particularly when previous experience has linked demand with pressure, unpredictability, or loss of control.

In environments that are noisy, changeable, or difficult to anticipate, the nervous system does not fully settle, and it remains oriented towards what might be required next, monitoring for interruption, demand, or shift. What is needed instead, such as steadiness, quiet, or predictability, is not always consistently available and in this state, the impact of demand is cumulative.

It is not only the individual request, but what it lands on- a system that is already activated does not receive demand in the same way as one that is at rest and when demands are repeatedly experienced in this way, the nervous system may begin to respond as though something unsafe is happening, even when the situation appears manageable from the outside.

Not About the Task Itself

The difficulty is often less about the task itself and more about the context in which it is introduced, and the way it arrives within the moment. A task that might feel manageable in one setting can become overwhelming in another, particularly when it is imposed rather than chosen, or when it interrupts something that is already in progress.

For many autistic people, engagement relies on a sense of continuity. Attention is not always easily redirected, and being interrupted can feel abrupt rather than flexible and, what is disrupted is not only the activity, but the internal state that made it possible to be there in the first place.

This can be confusing, both internally and externally and from the outside, it may appear inconsistent or irrational. From the inside, it reflects the difference between acting with a sense of autonomy and responding under pressure, where the same task carries a very different weight depending on how it is presented.

When Compliance Has a Cost

In many cases, compliance begins early, not as a conscious choice, but as a way of maintaining connection, avoiding conflict, or navigating environments where expectations are not easily adjusted.

Trying to meet those expectations, even at personal cost, can become a default pattern. What is needed internally may still be present, but it is gradually moved aside in favour of what is required externally, often without a clear awareness that this shift is happening and because this pattern can appear cooperative from the outside, the effort involved is rarely recognised.

Compliance is often read as willingness, when it is more accurately sustained effort, carried over long periods of time, sometimes with significant internal strain and what is less visible is the cumulative effect of repeatedly overriding internal signals. The cost does not always show immediately, but it builds in the background, shaping how much can be managed, how long things can be sustained, and how accessible a sense of ease remains.

When Resistance Becomes Necessary

What once felt manageable may begin to require more effort than can be sustained, and the strategies that previously allowed things to be tolerated no longer hold in the same way. This shift can feel abrupt, particularly when it follows a long period of appearing to cope, and it is often interpreted, both internally and externally, as something having gone wrong.

From the inside, however, the experience is different. It is not a loss of willingness, but the recognition, sometimes gradual and sometimes sudden, that a limit has been reached. Resistance emerges as a response that becomes harder to suppress, the body begins to push back where it has previously adapted, and what was once overridden becomes more difficult to ignore.

What was tolerated can no longer be sustained in the same way, and the shift that follows is less about change in character than a change in capacity. Seen in this light, resistance is not a failure to cope, but an indication that something within the current conditions is no longer workable.

Reframing Resistance

When resistance is understood as meaningful rather than problematic, the way it is approached begins to shift and instead of focusing only on the behaviour itself, attention moves toward what is being responded to and what, within the situation, may have become difficult to manage. What can appear, from the outside, as refusal or lack of cooperation often reflects a point at which something no longer feels tolerable, even if that is not immediately visible.

And so, resistance can be read as a form of communication, not always deliberate or clearly expressed, but nonetheless indicating that something within the current conditions is misaligned. It may point to pressure that has built gradually, to demands that feel disproportionate to capacity, or to a reduction in autonomy that has made engagement harder to sustain.

Approaching it in this way does not remove the difficulty, but it changes where understanding is directed. Rather than asking why someone will not comply, the question becomes more grounded in the conditions themselves and asks what feels unmanageable, what is being overridden, and where there is a need for more space, flexibility, or choice.

Autonomy as a Condition for Engagement

For many autistic people, the difference between being able to engage and being unable to is not simply the task itself, but whether there is a sense of autonomy within it.

For example, when something can be approached on one's own terms, with space to adjust pace, timing, or method, it often becomes far more manageable, even if the task itself has not changed. Yet, in contrast, the same demand, when imposed without flexibility or choice, can quickly become overwhelming, not because it is inherently difficult, but because it is experienced as pressure.

This does not mean that all demands can or should be avoided, but points to the way in which demands are encountered. When there is some degree of agency, whether through choice, collaboration, or the ability to pause and return, the nervous system is more able to remain settled enough for engagement to be possible.

Without that, the effort required is not only about completing the task, but about managing the internal impact of how it is being asked and this difference becomes significant, shaping not just what can be done, but how consistently and at what cost.

Moving Toward Autonomy

As awareness develops, there is often a gradual shift in how these experiences are understood, particularly in recognising the moments when something begins to feel like a demand rather than a choice although this does not necessarily mean that everything can be refused or avoided. In many situations, there are still practical limits, expectations, or responsibilities that cannot simply be removed, and there may be times when compliance continues to feel necessary.

What begins to change, however, is the ability to notice the internal response as it arises. A sense of pressure, a tightening, a pull away from what is being asked, or a disruption to an existing flow may start to register more clearly, not as something to immediately override, but as information that requires attention.

These signals start to become easier to recognise and differentiate and therefore it becomes possible to distinguish between what feels manageable, what requires adjustment, and what is likely to carry a cost if pushed through without consideration.

Even when action does not change immediately, the experience itself is no longer interpreted in the same way and what once felt like inconsistency, reluctance, or failure begins to make sense as a response to pressure, interruption, or reduced autonomy. The pattern becomes more visible, and with that visibility comes the possibility, not always immediate, but gradual, of responding differently.

Not Pathology, but Protection

When resistance is understood within this context, it begins to take on a different meaning and what might previously have been seen as a problem to fix or a behaviour to correct can be recognised instead as something that has developed for a reason. In environments and relational dynamics where autonomy has been limited or repeatedly overridden, resistance can emerge as a way of maintaining some degree of agency, even when that is not consciously intended.

Seen in this way, it is less about opposition and more about protection and as a response shaped over time, reflecting what has been difficult to sustain, rather than a reflection of unwillingness or defiance. This does not remove the challenges that can come with demands, expectations, or the realities of everyday life and those tensions remain but, what changes is the way they are understood, and with that, the way they are approached.

With greater understanding, there is often less blame directed inward. What once felt like being difficult, inconsistent, or uncooperative can begin to make sense as a response to pressure, to loss of control, or to conditions that required more than could reasonably be given.

In recognising this, the focus shifts away from trying to eliminate resistance, and toward understanding what it is responding to, and what might need to change for engagement to become possible again.

Chapter Seven: The Self That Was Not Allowed

When the Self Is Shaped Around Others

For those whose autism was not recognised early on, there is often a gradual realisation that who they are has been shaped in response to the needs, expectations, or emotional states of others.

This does not tend to happen in obvious or deliberate ways, it develops over time, through repeated adjustments where maintaining connection, avoiding conflict, or keeping the environment stable becomes more important than expressing what is internally felt. What is needed, expected, or acceptable begins to take priority, and responses are organised around meeting those demands.

In this process, the self is not explored so much as adapted. What feels natural, comfortable, or true may still be present, but it is often set aside, questioned, or overridden in favour of what works within the situation. Therefore, what forms is not an absence of self, but a pattern in which the self becomes flexible, responsive, and oriented around others, often at the expense of being recognised from within.

When Authenticity Carries Risk

In some environments, expressing yourself directly changes the atmosphere in ways that are not always spoken about but are nevertheless felt, in a shift of tone, a pause that lingers slightly too long, or a sense that something has landed wrong even when nothing has been said outright.

Certain ways of being seem to move through without friction, while others catch, and it is often through these small, repeated moments that an awareness begins to form around what can be expressed freely and what cannot.

Being open, emotional, resistant, or simply different can begin to carry a kind of weight, not always in ways that are easy to point to, but enough to be registered and remembered, shaping how the next moment is approached. There are also situations where the response is more immediate or more visible, where expression is met with frustration, criticism, or control, and where the impact is not only on what has been said or done, but on the sense of being oneself in that space.

Within these conditions, expression starts to narrow, with some responses softened, others filtered, and some held back entirely, as attention shifts away from what feels natural and toward what will pass without consequence. The self remains present throughout this, but its expression becomes shaped by where it has been met with ease and where it has not, so that what is felt internally is not always what is allowed to take form externally.

Relational Roles and Expectations

Certain ways of being begin to take shape, often quietly at first, then more consistently as they are reinforced by how others respond. What is noticed, accepted, or relied upon becomes clearer, and this gradually starts to organise how a person shows up in relationships.

There may be a movement toward becoming easier to be around, more accommodating, more aware of what others need, with attention shifting outward to read the room, anticipate reactions, and keep things steady. Not always consciously, but through repeated interactions where some responses seem to maintain connection while others create distance or tension.

This can take the form of recognisable roles:

The one who is easy.
The one who manages.
The one who understands others.
The one who does not need much.

These roles develop because they reduce friction, preserve connection, or prevent something more difficult from happening and become a way of staying within the relationship, particularly where acceptance feels uncertain or dependent on how well expectations are met.

Although this pattern often begins in early family environments, it does not remain there. Similar expectations can be encountered across friendships, education, workplaces, and intimate relationships, wherever there is a sense of what is acceptable and what is not. Across different contexts, the same question can begin to sit quietly underneath: what version of me will be received here?

The effort to meet those expectations can become deeply embedded, shaping not only behaviour, but the relationship to the self and there can be a strong pull toward maintaining harmony, avoiding rejection, and holding onto connection, even where this comes at a personal cost.

Because of this, certain aspects of the self are given more space, while others begin to recede and traits that are welcomed are expressed more readily. Those that are met with discomfort, criticism, or withdrawal tend to be softened, filtered, or set aside with heavy masking in many cases.

Due to this, what develops is a pattern in which some parts are lived more openly, while others remain less visible, carried more privately or only emerging in certain conditions and, the range of what is felt does not disappear, but the range of what can be expressed becomes narrower.

Underneath all of this is something very human which is the need for connection, the fear of being left and the sense that being fully oneself may risk distance, rejection, or loss. And so, adapting is not simply about fitting in but about being tied to belonging.

Enmeshment and Blurred Boundaries

In some relational dynamics, the boundaries between people are not clearly defined, and the line between what belongs to one person and what belongs to another becomes difficult to separate.

Emotional states, expectations, and responsibilities can begin to overlap in a way that makes responding to others feel immediate and, at times, unavoidable. What someone else feels can register as something that needs to be managed, steadied, or absorbed, often without it ever being named as such.

This kind of dynamic is often described as enmeshment, though it does not always present in obvious ways. It can sit within everyday interactions, where there is an ongoing awareness of shifts in mood, tone, or need and monitoring others can become automatic, less a decision and more a way of staying oriented within the environment.

Within this, it can become difficult to distinguish between one's own experience and that of others. A feeling may arise, but before it has been fully registered, it is already being adjusted in response to someone else and there can be a sense of responsibility for how others feel, even where that responsibility has not been explicitly given.

For autistic people, particularly where needs have not been recognised or supported, this kind of environment can be especially impactful. Sensitivity to emotional tone, combined with a learned need to adapt to maintain stability, can mean that these patterns become deeply embedded as a way of navigating situations that might otherwise feel unpredictable or overwhelming.

In these conditions, internal signals can become harder to access clearly. Preferences, limits, or discomfort may still be present, but they can be quieter, less certain, or more easily overridden, especially when they come into conflict with what is expected or needed by others.

The impact of this is not always immediately obvious. It can show up as a tendency to prioritise others automatically, difficulty identifying what is wanted or manageable, or a lingering sense of unease that is hard to trace back to a specific source.

For some, this pattern continues across different areas of life, extending into friendships, work, and intimate relationships, where similar dynamics are recreated without necessarily being recognised. A heightened awareness of others can begin to develop, not as a preference, but as something that feels necessary, with attention becoming finely tuned to shifts in mood, tone, and behaviour.

This kind of awareness of others is sometimes described as being highly empathic. While that may reflect how it feels, it is not always recognised that, for some, this sensitivity has been shaped in situations where staying attuned to others was closely linked to maintaining safety or stability and not some kind of natural, innate ability.

When emotional environments are unpredictable, intense, or difficult to read, becoming highly observant serves a purpose and quite often a need. It allows for adjustment of oneself before something escalates, or for anticipating what might be needed by another to prevent tension or disruption, anger or attack. And so, what appears as an innate sensitivity can also reflect a learned form of hypervigilance, where the nervous system remains oriented toward scanning and responding to others as a way of navigating uncertainty.

This does not make the sensitivity any less real. It places it within a context. Rather than being understood solely as a defining trait, it can also be seen as something that developed in response to conditions, where awareness of others became more immediately necessary than awareness of oneself.

What makes this particularly difficult to untangle is that stepping out of it does not happen in isolation. When someone has been relied upon to manage, accommodate, or absorb, any shift can be met with confusion, pressure, or resistance from others who are used to the dynamic being a certain way. The anxiety that may follow comes from anticipating those reactions, from knowing that changing the pattern may disrupt the dynamic, and from having to hold that tension while still trying to stay connected in a healthier, more authentic and balanced way.

Even so, recognising what has been happening begins to change the relationship to it by bringing a clearer sense of where one person ends, and another begins. This may show up first in small moments such as a pause before reacting, a flicker of hesitation, a sense that something does not quite sit right. The pattern may continue but it is no longer entirely invisible to oneself and from there, a different kind of movement becomes possible. Not a complete shift, but the gradual untangling of what has been carried, what is not yours to hold or fix, where responses to others are no longer the same, and where there is, slowly, the possibility of returning to one's own experience as something that can be noticed, held, prioritised and acted upon.

Parentification and Reversed Roles

In some families, there is no consistent sense of calm or stability coming from the adult and so life can feel unpredictable without there being anyone safe and steady to return to. There is no conscious sense of needing to get through or endure as a child, but an experience of continuing on day by day shaped by the surroundings, often with very little support for what is felt or needed, and with no clear sense of whether that support might arrive.

There is no clear understanding of what is happening at the time, only the experience of living within it, resulting in frustration that does not settle, anger that has nowhere to go, and a sense of being unsettled, irritated, or on edge without any relief. These emotional experiences are not subtle and are overwhelming, confusing, and at times consuming, with different feelings sitting alongside each other such as anger, sadness, loneliness, and resentment without a way to separate or make sense of them.

In home environments that are loud, chaotic, or unpredictable, the impact of constant noise, disruption, and the absence of quiet or routine can make it difficult to settle, to sleep, or to feel at ease within the space. The body reacts to this, even when there is no language for it, and the result is often stress related ailments, exhaustion, tension, and being in a constant state of alertness created by what is happening around.

There can also be a kind of knowing that something is not as it should be, even without being able to explain it, arecognition that what is needed is not what is being provided, and that the environment does not feel supportive in the way it needs to.

Because of this, the adult's emotional state comes to shape the atmosphere in a way that cannot be ignored, and gradually there is a pulling toward adjusting around it, even without fully understanding why.

There is no space to be carefree in a state of constant hypervigilance and anxiety, and the child is constantly aware of what might be required next, in not being able to fully settle into play or rest, in carrying a background sense of needing to stay attuned. For an autistic child, this can be particularly destabilising, because what is needed most is consistency, predictability, and a sense of safety, and instead they find themselves in a situation that feels uncertain, intense, or difficult to read.

In that kind of setting, the nervous system does not get the chance to settle and it stays in a state of fight or flight, tuned to what is happening, holding a level of responsibility that does not match what a child can reasonably carry, so that rest is not just about being still, but about whether it feels safe to stop monitoring, and often it does not.

From the outside, individuals who experience this childhood end up as the adult who understands, who supports, who seems capable and aware, yet what is being seen is only one side of it, because underneath that is the absence of support for their own experience, and the pressure of holding something that was never meant to be theirs. There is a continued sense of responsibility toward the parent, a feeling that their needs take priority, and that stepping back would result in not being viewed as a good person by themselves or others.

It also shapes other relationships, where being the one who listens, understands, and holds things together becomes expected, and where value can begin to feel tied to what is offered rather than to simply being present. Relationships can form around that dynamic, drawing in people who rely on that steadiness, who come for support, and who assume it will continue without boundaries and those who may take advantage of the openness and understanding on offer.

At the same time, when support is needed from other adults in return, it may not be there and this can bring a sense of being too much, or of becoming a burden at the point where strength can no longer be maintained. This then reiterates the experience from childhood and what is visible to others is the capacity to give, while what is missed is the need to receive.

Gradually, value can become linked to how much is carried, your strength and perceived wisdom, how much can be managed and, how well others are supported, until it becomes difficult to separate who you are from what you do for other people.

When The Self Is Constrained

Under these conditions, the self does not disappear, but it begins to narrow in how it can be lived and expressed externally.

Some of the natural ways of being seem to be acceptable to others and are met with ease or acceptance, comeing forward more often, while other aspects meet something different, such as tension, correction, dismissal, or a subtle shift in connection, and slowly, almost without being noticed, those parts begin to be held back. It does not happen all at once, and there is no clear moment where it begins, but through small, repeated adjustments, a pattern forms around what feels safe to show and what is better left unexpressed.

Nothing about this feels deliberate. It takes shape through experience, through noticing what settles the situation and what unsettles it, and learning, often very early, how to stay within what keeps things steady.

Expression itself begins to change, and communication becomes more careful, more filtered, sometimes more contained, with an increasing awareness that saying the wrong thing can shift how others respond.

In certain situations, especially where there is pressure or too much to process at once, words can become difficult to reach altogether. Many autistic people recognise moments like this, where speech drops away, whether briefly, in particular environments, or for longer periods, not because language is absent, but because everything around it has become too much to hold and respond to at the same time.

In those moments, silence can feel safer, not in a conscious or chosen way, but because it reduces the chance of getting something wrong, of being misunderstood, or of drawing attention in a way that might lead to correction or discomfort. It steadies things enough to get through, but it also means less of what is there internally finds a way out, and gradually this shapes how the self is lived, not just outwardly, but in how it comes to be experienced from within.

There can still be a sense, somewhere underneath it all, of what is felt more fully, reactions, needs, ways of being that do not quite fit into what is expressed, but there is less space for them to take form. What develops is not an absence of self, but a version of it that becomes organised around what can exist without creating disharmony externally.

It can begin to feel as though life is being lived within limits that were never consciously chosen, where certain responses stay held back, certain needs remain unspoken, and certain ways of being feel just out of reach, not because they are not there, but because they have not had the conditions needed to exist safely and there is an inner disharmony that forms as a consequence.

Even when something is not expressed, it does not disappear but it continues quietly, shaping reactions, influencing patterns, sitting just beneath what is visible, so that the range of what is felt remains, while the range of what can be lived becomes narrower, leaving a quiet sense that something is being held or not fully reached, even within oneself.

The Cost of Constriction

Living in this way takes far more energy than it appears from the outside.

There is a constant effort running underneath everything, in tracking what is happening around you, adjusting in response to it, and maintaining a version of yourself that fits what the situation seems to require. It is there in the small pauses before speaking, in the filtering of responses, in the decisions that happen so quickly they are barely noticed, all shaping what is expressed and what stays contained.

That effort does not switch off. It continues in the background, creating a sense of always being slightly on alert, as though something needs to be monitored or managed, even in moments that are meant to feel ordinary or at ease. This can become deeply tiring, in a way that is hard to fully explain, because so much of it sits beneath what is visible.

Alongside this, a kind of distance can begin to form within. There may be a clear sense of what is felt, of what matters, of how things are experienced internally, yet far less opportunity for that to take shape outwardly and it can feel like holding something in place for long periods, where expression is limited, responses are contained, and parts of yourself remain just beneath the surface.

Moving Toward Expression

As this way of living becomes more visible to oneself, something begins to shift and there is a growing recognition of what has been happening, of how much has been adapted, managed, or held back to keep things steady and acceptable for others. That recognition does not arrive as clarity straight away but often comes in waves with hesitation, with second-guessing, with an awareness that expressing more fully may still result in uncomfortable situations.

There can be a sense of standing in between two ways of being. One that is the old and familiar, shaped around what is expected, and another that feels closer to what is truly authentic, but less practised, less certain, and at times more exposed. Moving toward honest expression and beginning to say and do what feels right for you is not a clean or confident step forward. It is difficult, often confusing, uncertain and sometimes only noticeable in small moments where something is said that would previously have been held back, or where a response is no longer shaped entirely around what will keep things easy for others.

These moments begin to show that something else is possible, and that there is not a complete change, but a loosening of the old ways of being.

The Self That Remained

What begins to emerge at this stage does not feel like something new being created but more like something that has been there all along, now given a little more space to exist without apology.

There may still be inconsistency, moments of clarity followed by moments of hesitation, a sense of moving forward and then stepping back again. Confident self-expression does not suddenly become easy or natural but there is a difference in how it feels with less behaviour driven by what is required, and more connected to what is personally experienced and felt within.

This can bring a paradox of both relief and discomfort. Relief in recognising that the self was never lost, only constrained and that it is time to live life for you, within your limits without apology. Discomfort in realising how much has been shaped around others, how much time has been lost and how many opportunities may have been missed, as well as how unfamiliar it can feel to move outside of old patterns.

What takes shape here, in these early moments of awareness, is not a finished or fully expressed version of the self, but a shift in direction. A gradual movement toward living in a way that is less organised around expectation of others, and more anchored in internal experience, even if that process remains ongoing and, at times, uncertain.

Chapter Eight: Living Without Justification

When Explanation Becomes Habit

A tendency to explain in detail is present among many autistic people, with answers becoming longer than the question requires, with context, reasoning, and clarification woven in, which develops through repeated experiences of being misunderstood, of having words taken out of context, or of finding that what was said has been reshaped into something else entirely. Therefore, explanation becomes a way of trying to stay accurate, to make sure that meaning is not lost or altered once it leaves you.

In practice, this can mean responding carefully and thoroughly, filling in gaps before they can be misread, and attempting to anticipate how something might be interpreted. A simple exchange can turn into something more long-winded and complex because the aim is not just to answer, but to be understood as intended. It can also show up as a need to justify, to defend, or to explain fully enough that there is little room left for misinterpretation, even when that level of detail is not actually being asked for.

With such effort, it can be met with irritation, impatience or dismissal by others. What is offered to create clarity may be experienced by others as unnecessary or excessive, particularly in environments where communication differences are not recognised or taken seriously. This can be especially pronounced in interactions with professionals not just in personal relationships, where there is already a sense of needing to be precise, and where being misunderstood carries real consequences. Despite this, the explaining continues, because leaving things unsaid has its own history, and that history carries weight.

The Pressure to Be Understood

Alongside the habit of explaining, there can be a persistent sense that understanding depends on how well something is communicated, as though clarity sits entirely in the wording, the tone, and the way something is presented. What is felt internally begins to be shaped into something more acceptable before it is even spoken, with language adjusted, edges softened, and meaning carefully organised in the hope that it will land as intended.

This can bring a constant awareness of how something might be received, where attention is not only on what is being said, but on how it will be interpreted, whether it might be dismissed, and how it could be made more understandable in advance. It becomes less about simple expression and more about managing the conditions around it, with the underlying assumption that if something is said carefully enough, thoroughly enough, and in the right way, it will eventually be recognised.

Holding this requires ongoing effort and asks for attention to detail, restraint, and a level of self monitoring that does not switch off, particularly in situations where being misunderstood carries consequences. The pressure is not always visible from the outside, but it sits quietly underneath the interaction, shaping how much is said, how it is said, and how much is held back.

When Explanation Does Not Lead to Recognition

At a certain point, a different understanding begins to take shape through repeated experiences where this constant careful communication does not change the outcome anyway. There are situations where something is explained clearly and still minimised, where boundaries are expressed and still questioned, and where meaning is made explicit yet received in a different form.

Part of that recognition is more difficult to sit with. It includes the realisation that some people are not going to meet what is being said, not because it has not been explained well enough, but because they are not approaching it from a place of curiosity or openness. The difference in experience is not taken seriously, or is filtered through assumptions about what is normal, reasonable, or correct, leaving little room for a genuinely different way of being to be recognised as valid in its own right.

Sitting with this can feel confronting, particularly when so much energy has gone into trying to communicate clearly and carefully. It brings into view a limit that is not within your control, where understanding is not something that can be secured through effort alone, and where continuing to explain does not change what is, or is not, being met.

Internal Permission

Instead of everything needing to be explained, justified, or agreed with to feel valid, something begins to settle more internally, where experience is recognised as real without requiring it to be translated into something that will be accepted by someone else.

It can feel unfamiliar to stop explaining, or to allow something to stand without adding context around it, particularly when there has been a long-standing pattern of needing to make things clear and to be taken seriously. There can still sometimes be a pull to go back into explaining, to soften what is said, or to check whether it has been received in the right way.

What begins to change is not the desire to be understood, but the sense that understanding from others is what determines whether something is allowed to exist. Feelings, limits, and preferences start to be recognised as valid in themselves, even when they are not agreed with, or when they are not fully understood by the person on the other side.

This can bring a different kind of steadiness as less energy is directed toward trying to secure recognition, and more toward staying connected to what is felt as true and right from within. Decisions begin to come from that place, even if they are not always explained in detail, and even if they are not always received well externally.

Holding that position can still feel uncomfortable at times, particularly in relationships, within dynamics or environments where explanation has been expected. The difference is that the discomfort is no longer managed by overriding what is known internally, but by allowing it to be there while remaining aligned with it.

Letting a Boundary Stand

Boundaries can begin to shift in how they are held, moving away from something that needs to be explained, justified, or negotiated repeatedly, and becoming more internally known and trusted. There is a growing sense of where a limit sits, even if it is not always expressed clearly or confidently, and even if it is not always received well by others.

This does not mean boundaries suddenly become easy to communicate and it can still feel uncomfortable to allow something to stand without softening it, particularly when there has been a long history of adjusting to keep things calm or to avoid tension. The instinct to explain, to reassure, or to make something easier for the other person does not disappear straight away, and there may still be moments where that instinct takes over.

There are times when it feels easier to step back into what is familiar, especially when energy is low or when the situation carries pressure. Agreeing, accommodating, or smoothing things over can feel like the simplest way through in that moment, even when it comes at a personal cost and these moments do not undo what is being learned, but they can bring into view just how established those patterns have been, and how much practice it takes to respond differently.

What begins to change is the relationship to that pattern. There is more awareness of when something does not feel right, violates a personal boundary and evokes feelings of irritation and anger at times with a growing ability to recognise those feeling without overriding them. Boundaries start to take shape from that place, gradually becoming easier to hold, even if they are still not expressed confidently or with ease.

Letting a boundary stand can bring discomfort, particularly when it is not accepted or when it creates tension in a relationship that has been used to a different dynamic. Sitting with that discomfort is part of the shift and the boundary does not need to disappear to restore ease, and it does not require agreement from the other person to remain valid.

The Discomfort of Not Explaining

Stepping back from the need to explain can feel unfamiliar at first, particularly when explanation has been relied on for so long as a way of maintaining connection or avoiding being misunderstood.

There can be a pull to fill the silence, to add more context, or to make something clearer, even when experience has shown that clarity is not always what is missing but understanding of a different way of being.

Alongside this comes an awareness of how it may be received by those used to old dynamics and there may be an underlying feeling at first about being seen as difficult or abrupt, especially in relationships where explanation and compliance have been expected. In those moments, choosing not to expand can feel exposing and uncomfortable but necessary to maintain boundaries in a clear, direct and firm way.

There is also the recognition that explanation does not always lead to being heard. When something has repeatedly been dismissed, minimised, or reshaped by the other person, continuing to explain can begin to feel less like communication and more like an effort that goes nowhere. Letting go of that effort can bring a different kind of discomfort as well as a sense of freedom, one that comes from allowing that reality to stand rather than trying to change it.

Not Everything Requires Defence

With this new awareness, something begins to shift in how explanation is used. There is less urgency to justify every decision or to translate every internal experience into something that will be accepted by others, and more space to allow certain things to remain as they are, even if they are not fully understood by anyone but yourself.

This does not mean withdrawing or becoming closed off to connection, it is more of a quiet change in where responsibility sits, where communication is no longer used to secure permission or to prevent disagreement, but to express what feels true when it is appropriate to do so. Some things are shared; others are simply held.

Self-Trust Without Certainty

Self-trust tends to show up subtly and gradually with the willingness to take internal signals seriously, even when they are incomplete, difficult to explain, or still forming.

There can be a shift from needing to fully understand a feeling before acting on it, toward recognising that something matters simply because it is felt within. Decisions may begin to come from that place, without the same level of justification that once felt necessary, and without waiting for everything to make logical sense first.

Part of this also involves a change in where decisions are sourced from where previously there may have been a strong pull to seek advice, reassurance, to ask others what they think, or to gather perspectives in the hope that something will feel clearer and make more sense.

While insight from others can be valuable, it can also become confusing when it begins to replace rather than support internal awareness, especially when those perspectives are shaped by experiences that are different from one's own. What begins to matter more is not the absence of outside input, but the ability to return to oneself within it, to notice what resonates and what does not.

At times, this can feel uncertain and there may be doubt, or a sense of not quite being able to put something into words, particularly when so much of the past has involved explaining, clarifying, or making things acceptable to others. Even so, something begins to settle internally, where the absence of a clear explanation does not automatically mean that a decision is wrong.

Holding a boundary or making a choice in this way can feel rather alien, yet it also brings a different kind of steadiness and freedom with emphasis less on how something is received, and more in whether it feels right from within.

A Subtle Shift

The shift is not always obvious from the outside as what has changed sits more in how experience is held within, than in what is visibly expressed; so, it may look as though little is different, even when something significant has shifted internally.

There is less pressure to reshape what is felt into something that will be understood, and less urgency to correct or expand in anticipation of how it might be received. Because this change is internal, it does not always meet recognition and others may continue to respond in familiar ways, interpreting or questioning from the same perspective as before. The shift, then, is not in how things are received, but in how much that response determines what happens next.

Not Always Comfortable, but More Accurate

Living in this newfound way does not remove discomfort and there can still be misunderstanding, or moments where something is questioned, dismissed, or met without the depth that was hoped for. The difference is in what happens internally in response to that.

Where there was once a pull to adjust, explain further, or move away from what felt true to restore ease, there is now more capacity to remain with it, even when it creates tension. That tension does not disappear, but it no longer carries the same authority, and any discomfort or ill feeling is left with the other person as the awareness that it is not yours to hold dawns.

What begins to take its place is a quieter form of steadiness and self-trust and a sense of staying closer to one's own experience, even when it is not reflected back or understood externally. And so, life becomes less organised around being validated, and more around recognising and responding to what is already known to be right from within.

Chapter Nine: The Cost of Authenticity

When Authenticity Changes the Landscape

As internal experience becomes harder to ignore, the way decisions are made begins to shift. What once felt manageable through adjustment or compliance no longer settles in the same way, and there is a growing pull to respond differently, even in situations that have long followed a familiar pattern.

This emerges in smaller moments, in pausing before agreeing, in noticing when something feels misaligned, or in choosing not to move past that feeling as quickly as before and what changes is not only what is said or done, but the point from which those responses come.

At first, these shifts can be difficult to define. They may show up as leaving earlier than expected, taking longer to respond, or not stepping into roles that were once taken on without question and, from the outside, this can appear subtle or inconsistent. From within, it often feels more deliberate, even when the reasons are not fully articulated.

What begins to change is the structure of how life is organised. There is less automatic movement toward what keeps things smooth, and more attention given to what is manageable, sustainable, or true to experience. This does not necessarily make things easier, but it does make them more aligned, and that alignment starts to carry its own weight.

When Familiar Patterns No Longer Hold

As awareness deepens and behaviour begins to change, the patterns that once shaped relationships do not simply fade. They are still there, still expected, and pulling you in the same direction, but something in you no longer meets them in the same way, and that is where the tension begins.

What came before was endurance, adjustment, holding things in place without fully understanding why it felt so heavy and overwhelming. There was a sense of carrying something that did not belong to you, without the language to name it or the ability to step out of it and that experience does not disappear; it becomes clearer.

Once that clarity arrives, it cannot be undone and every day interactions begin to look different. There is an increasing awareness of what is being asked for beneath the surface, of how certain responses once kept things steady, even when they came at a personal cost. The difficulty is that the dynamic itself often remains unchanged, and so the pressure to return to what was familiar continues.

In some relationships, this becomes an ongoing point of conflict rather than something that settles and holding boundaries is not a single moment, but something that must be maintained repeatedly, often in the face of resistance, unkindness, and pushback. When the other person has not shifted in their awareness, the same expectations continue, and the same patterns are still being reached for, even though you are no longer willing, or able, to step into them.

There can be a sense of being caught between what is now seen clearly and what is still being asked for. Each interaction may carry a need to stay aware, to think carefully about what is said and what may follow, to avoid being pulled back into dynamics that once went unchallenged but are no longer tolerable. It is not a clean transition into something new, but an ongoing effort to remain aligned with what you now recognise as true.

At times, the urge to withdraw or escape can feel strong in the face of exhaustion of holding that line repeatedly. It takes energy to stay steady in the face of reactions that do not meet you where you are, especially when there is a growing recognition that the other person may not be willing or able to change and may continue as they always have.

This is part of the cost of awareness and the clarity that develops brings with it a different kind of weight, because once something is understood, it continues to shape how everything else is experienced.

Being Seen Differently

When long-standing patterns begin to shift, the way a person is perceived often changes alongside them, though not in a way that reflects what is taking place beneath the surface.

A person who was once consistently available may now be described as distant, and someone who rarely expressed limits can be seen as abrupt or unkind when those limits begin to take shape. What is happening internally is a movement toward clarity and self-respect, yet it is often read externally as withdrawal or a change in character, as though something has gone wrong rather than something being recognised.

In some relationships, this brings resistance rather than understanding, because the roles that once existed are still being expected, even when they are no longer being met. When that expectation is disrupted, there can be a steady pressure to return to what was familiar, sometimes through guilt, sometimes through emotional reactions that position the other person as affected or overlooked, and sometimes through quieter attempts to re-establish the same dynamic without it being named directly.

This becomes more pronounced in close family relationships, where expectations are often less visible but more deeply embedded. There can be an underlying assumption that access, availability, or emotional support are simply part of the role, and that these things do not require negotiation. When boundaries begin to appear, they are not always recognised as something necessary that has developed through experience, but can instead be perceived as something personal, an attack, abandonment and something directed at the person themselves.

It can create a strange contradiction, where the idea of having boundaries is accepted in general, even encouraged, yet becomes difficult to tolerate when it is applied within the relationship. The same limits that are considered reasonable elsewhere may be resisted, questioned, or quietly worked around when they are brought closer to home. Attempts to regain influence can take different forms, including vulnerability, suggestion, or gestures that create a sense of obligation, making it harder to remain steady without feeling drawn back into what once felt unavoidable.

From within, there is usually a clear awareness of what is happening. Patterns that once went unnoticed become visible, including ways of relating that involve pressure, expectation, or a shaping of responses over time. Once seen, these patterns do not disappear, and continuing as before begins to feel increasingly difficult, even when the alternative requires more effort.

From the outside, however, this shift is rarely understood in those terms. It is more often interpreted as a change in you, rather than a response to an inappropriate dynamic that has been present for far too long. The focus remains on how you are now behaving, rather than on what has led to that change, which can leave you holding an understanding that is not shared.

This is where the difficulty lies, because you are no longer able to move through these dynamics without awareness, yet the expectation that you will do so may remain. What follows is not a clean break, but an ongoing job, where maintaining boundaries requires attention, energy, and a willingness to face responses that do not reflect your experience or needs, even when you can see clearly where they come from.

The Loss of Familiar Roles

Letting go of roles that have been held for much of a lifetime can bring a quiet sense of loss, even when those roles were never freely chosen. They often provided a kind of structure, shaping how relationships functioned and how connection was maintained, even when carrying them felt heavy.

There is often a familiar position that develops over time, the one who manages, who holds things together, who is steady, organised, and able to make sense of what others bring. It can become something others rely on without question, turning to that person for advice, reassurance, or clarity, until it begins to feel as though that is where their place sits within the relationship.

Stepping back from that position is not always straightforward. There may be a growing recognition that holding other people's emotional weight, offering constant support, or being the one who has the answers is not something that belongs to them, yet the habit of responding in that way can remain, particularly in moments where it feels easier to return to what is familiar than to hold a different position.

Without that role, there can be a period where things feel less defined and the structure it once provided begins to loosen, and in its place, there is space that does not immediately feel settled. Questions can begin to surface, not always clearly, but persistently enough to be felt.

Who am I if I am not the one who manages?
Who am I if I am not the one who is always available?

These questions do not tend to resolve quickly, especially when the role that is being stepped away from has shaped not only relationships, but a sense of identity.

There is also a complexity in recognising that some aspects of that role may still feel natural. Being thoughtful, organised, or able to see things clearly may not feel entirely separate from the self, yet those qualities may have developed alongside a need to adapt to instability or chaos.

Untangling what is inherent from what was required can take time, particularly when both have been lived as one.

This can leave a sense of standing in between, no longer fully stepping into the role that once defined things, but not yet fully grounded in something new. The patterns that developed early do not disappear immediately and may still show up in moments where energy is low or the situation feels difficult to navigate, even when there is a clear awareness that they are no longer needed in the same way.

When Connection Changes

As alignment with internal experience strengthens, the nature of connection begins to shift in ways that are difficult to ignore. Relationships that were once maintained through adjustment, tolerance, or a quiet overlooking of what felt wrong begin to feel strained, as participation in those dynamics changes and can no longer be sustained in the same way.

Awareness sharpens around what has been present within relationships for a long time, including patterns that once felt familiar but carried an underlying imbalance. Dynamics built on one person giving more, adapting more, or holding more start to become visible, and when that effort is no longer given automatically, the structure of the relationship itself is exposed.

Some connections deepen where there is space for honesty, difference, and a willingness to meet more equally. Others begin to loosen or fall away as it becomes clear what the relationship can and cannot hold. Distance may be created deliberately, contact reduced, or ties ended where patterns feel repetitive, harmful, or resistant to change.

There are also relationships that remain in place, where awareness has shifted but the dynamic itself continues largely unchanged. These require careful navigation, with boundaries held more consistently, less shared, and a growing acceptance of the limits within that connection, rather than a continued effort to reshape it.

Alongside this comes a clearer recognition of personal patterns, including being drawn toward relationships that echo earlier experiences. But that familiarity begins to lose its pull as those patterns become more visible, and responses shift, even when old instincts still surface at times and discernment becomes stronger.

The behaviour of others that once would have been explained or excused away is noticed earlier, and there is less willingness to remain in situations that feel misaligned. Decisions to step back, disengage, or avoid certain people are made more readily, grounded in a clearer sense of what is and is not acceptable.

The way of relating often becomes more selective and a smaller number of relationships feel more sustainable, particularly those that allow for steadiness, mutuality, and ease. Solitude can begin to feel more aligned than environments that require constant adjustment, with a quiet return to what has always felt more natural.

What begins to take shape is a way of relating and interacting that no longer centres on maintaining connection at any cost, but on recognising where connection is beneficial, balanced, and fulfilling and where it is limited, unbalanced and causing harm or distress.

A Different Kind of Steadiness

A kind of steadiness begins to take shape, one that comes less from keeping things consistent on the outside and more from a quieter sense of internal clarity. There may still be change, and there may still be uncertainty, but the tension that once sat between what is felt and what is expressed begins to ease, so that responses feel less forced and to please others, and more aligned with internal truth.

As patterns become clearer, there is a shift in how situations are understood and responded to, and what once felt confusing or overwhelming begins to settle into something more recognisable. Decisions are no longer guided in the same way by how they might be received, or by the need to maintain ease with others, and instead begin to follow a steadier internal reference point that develops gradually and becomes easier to trust.

With that, there is often a change in how input from others is held. Insight can still be valuable, and connection can still matter, but it no longer carries the same weight in shaping decisions and does not replace what is known from within. There is less pulling away from oneself to accommodate what others might think or expect, and more ability to remain with what feels true, even when that creates difficulty.

Relationships may still bring tension, and there may be moments where boundaries are met with resistance, or where firmness feels uncomfortable to hold. What shifts is the internal experience of those moments, where there is less confusion about what is happening, and less inclination to question or override what has already been recognised. At times, when there is a response of being minimised or dismissed, you recognise it for what it is, acknowledge it within and decide not to react because that response you received is more about the other person and how they feel within about themselves, than about you.

Care, compassion, and responsibility remain where appropriate, but they are no longer carried when they are not yours to hold. There is a clearer sense of what belongs to oneself and what does not, and a growing steadiness in holding that distinction without needing to justify it or soften it to maintain connections.

This creates a form of security that does not depend on everything around being stable or predictable all the time. It comes instead from a deeper trust in one's own responses, limits, and choices, so that even where external dynamics remain unsettled, there is a greater sense of being grounded within.

Chapter Ten: Grieving What Was Not Lived

When Understanding Arrives Later

For many autistic people diagnosed later in life, understanding does not arrive alongside the experiences it relates to. You have a sense of not fitting in, of things not feeling right, or of not being able to keep up with peers. The understanding comes after diagnosis, and through personal research, when much of life has already been lived without a framework to make sense of it.

Experiences that once felt confusing begin to take on a different meaning as patterns become more visible, and responses that were questioned or pathologised start to make sense within a context that had been missing. There is a sense of relief and more self-compassion for the things you have done in the past, the poor decisions you may have made and the inability to meet societal standards or keep up with peers. Now, with a diagnosis there is recognition that there was a reason for all this, and that what was experienced was never without context.

At the same time, this clarity brings attention to how long these experiences went unsupported, judged and how often they were interpreted through frameworks that did not reflect what was actually taking place.

The Shape of What Was Missed

With this understanding comes greater understanding of what was not available at the time, including support that was never offered, needs that went unrecognised, and explanations that were replaced with labels that did not reflect the underlying reality. In many cases, particularly for women, the explanations for struggles and difficulty in early adult life were incorrect and misdiagnoses of labels such as borderline personality disorder, bipolar and anxiety and depression are given, without recognition of the underlying autistic experience that presents differently in women.

A stark contrast begins to form between what was lived and what might have been possible under different conditions, where earlier recognition may have changed how experiences were understood, how support was accessed, and how identity formed in relation to those experiences. You may wonder if you might have done better in school, performed well within your job role, would have been able to reach your full potential if only you had been seen and supported in the way you needed.

There may be a mix of grief and anger in this, directed not only at those closest to you but also systems or professionals and toward the absence of questions that were never asked. The weight of the reality of the persistence required to keep seeking help without being met in a way that led to the right answers is infuriating and carries a sense of having had to navigate life without the information that would have made those experiences more coherent at the time.

Protection that was not provided.

With greater understanding can come a clearer sense of what was needed at the time, and how differently experiences might have unfolded if those needs had been recognised and responded to. What is often missing is not only practical support, but a way of being met that allows experience to be understood rather than questioned or dismissed.

There may have been a need for patience, for space to think and respond, for questions that explored rather than corrected, and for limits to be acknowledged without pressure to move past them. Ways of seeing and processing that differed from those around may have been treated as problems to fix, rather than as differences that could be worked with and understood and, in a different context, those same ways of thinking might have been recognised as strengths, offering depth, insight, or a different perspective that adds value rather than needing to be contained.

This absence of understanding often extends beyond early life into wider systems that continue to prioritise a narrow definition of what is considered capable or successful. Environments such as education and employment can be structured around expectations that favour social ease, adaptability, and constant availability, leaving little room for different ways of functioning and, opportunities may be missed because the conditions required to access or sustain them are not available.

There can be a sense that what is offered is not designed with autistic people in mind, where the emphasis is placed on fitting into existing structures rather than shaping those structures to accommodate different needs. This can make it difficult to use strengths in a way that is sustainable, particularly where expectations involve long hours, constant interaction, or managing multiple demands at once.

With greater awareness and insight, there could be more recognition of individual skill sets, with space to focus on areas of strength without the same pressure to meet every aspect of a role. Working patterns that allow for consistency and recovery, alongside a reduced emphasis on constant social engagement, could make participation more accessible and sustainable and so, rather than being seen as a limitation, autistic difference could be understood as something that contributes to society in its own unique way.

Because this was not, and is still largely not in place, the result can be a sense of being overlooked or misunderstood and having potential that has gone to waste where the focus remains on what is difficult about autism rather than what is possible. The absence of protection is not always visible, yet it shapes what is able to develop, what is supported, and what is missed.

Grief Without a Clear Event

There can be the kind of grief that does not sit neatly within a single moment or memory. It is not tied to one experience that can be pointed to, but to a way of moving through life that developed gradually, often without awareness, and without the understanding that comes with a later autism diagnosis.

Because this understanding arrives afterwards, there is no clear beginning to the grief, and no clear ending either, it does not move through in a defined sequence or resolve in a single moment and it can surface quietly, in reflection, in a growing awareness of what was lived without being recognised for what it was at the time.

As the lens of autism is applied to earlier experiences, there can be a tendency to move back through memories and see them completely differently. Situations that once felt confusing, personal, or difficult to explain begin to make sense within this new context, and connections start to form between experiences giving greater clarity of why and how things unfolded as they did.

This can bring a recognition of how far that influence reaches. It is not limited to isolated events, but touches relationships, responses, and ways of coping that developed across years without being understood. And so, what emerges is a sense of something that has been present throughout, shaping experience in ways that were never fully visible at the time.

The process of looking back in this way can feel overwhelming and heavy but also enlightening. It is less about arriving at a final understanding, more about gradually seeing more of what was already there and recognising the extent to which the impact of undiagnosed autism has been woven through it.

Not About Blame, but Recognition

As understanding develops, there can also be a growing awareness of the context in which these experiences took place and for many autistic people, particularly girls, the recognition that is now more widely discussed simply was not present in the same way at the time. Awareness of how autism can present outside of more visible or stereotypical forms was limited, and in many settings, it was not something that was actively considered.

In environments such as schools, workplaces, and healthcare, there was often a lack of understanding around how autistic traits might appear, especially where they were less obvious or expressed differently. Professionals were working within the knowledge available to them, and that knowledge did not always include the full range of autistic experience. As a result, what was seen was interpreted through frameworks that were more familiar, even when they did not fully fit.

Although, recognising this does not remove what was experienced and it does not change the absence of support, the missed opportunities for understanding, or the impact of being repeatedly misunderstood. There can still be a clear sense of having been let down, not only in the past but in ways that continue where awareness has yet to reach the places it is needed.

It is possible for both realities to exist at once and there can be an understanding of the limitations that were present, alongside anger at the consequences of those limitations. One does not cancel out the other and the wider context can be acknowledged without dismissing the personal impact, and the absence of blame does not require the absence of recognition.

The Loss of Time

Alongside greater understanding, there can be a growing awareness of time that has already passed, and of how much of that time was shaped by circumstances that were not fully recognised or understood. This is not only about a later diagnosis, but about the combination of factors that influenced how life was lived, including patterns such as parentification and enmeshment that placed responsibility in places it did not belong.

There can be a sense that large parts of life were spent responding to others, adjusting to expectations, or managing dynamics that required constant effort, leaving little room for anything to develop in a way that felt chosen. What becomes clearer is not just that this happened, but how long it went on for, and how much of it was carried without the language or awareness to question it.

That realisation can bring a sharper kind of anger, not only at what was missed, but at the extent to which it was taken for granted that this was simply how things were. It is not only about opportunities that were not available, but about the years spent living in ways that were shaped around others, where personal needs, timing, and direction were repeatedly set aside.

With that comes a sense of time having been lost in a way that cannot be recovered. Understanding may arrive, patterns may become clear, and change may begin, but it does not alter the fact that those years have already been lived.

There can be a recognition that certain experiences may now feel more difficult to access, or carry a different weight, because of when this clarity has arrived.

At times, this awareness turns toward the future with a sense of urgency or concern, particularly where there are limits that cannot be ignored, or where the path that was once expected no longer feels possible in the same way. These thoughts do not always settle easily, especially where they sit alongside the knowledge of how much effort it has taken to reach this point.

At the same time, the present holds its own reality. The process of understanding, untangling, and responding differently has required sustained effort, particularly where patterns were established early and reinforced over time. What may look like delay from the outside reflects the depth of what has been navigated, and the work involved in reaching a place where choices can begin to feel more aligned.

The loss that sits here does not disappear. It can remain present in different ways, sometimes more sharply, sometimes more quietly, as part of an ongoing awareness of what was shaped by circumstance, and what cannot be returned to or rewritten.

What Cannot Be Rewritten

As understanding deepens, there often comes a point where it becomes clear that the past cannot be returned to or reshaped, even when it is now seen differently. Earlier experiences may make more sense, patterns may be recognised, and their impact may be understood with a clarity that was not available at the time, yet none of this changes how those years were lived.

There can be a sense of holding what did not happen alongside what did, including opportunities that were never available, paths that were shaped by circumstance rather than choice, and parts of life that unfolded within dynamics that could not be stepped out of at the time. This can feel particularly present where a later autism diagnosis brings new understanding to earlier experiences, and where family dynamics placed responsibility or expectation in ways that limited what was possible.

What is felt here is not only about specific moments, but about the presence of something that was never able to fully take shape. It may appear as a quiet awareness of how things might have been different under other conditions, or as a recognition of needs, directions, or ways of being that did not have the space to develop.

There is no way to return to those points and live them differently and that realisation can sit heavily at times, particularly when it becomes clear that certain paths are no longer available in the same way or would now carry a different weight.

What begins to shift is not the past itself, but the relationship to it and rather than trying to recover what cannot be lived in its original form, there can be a gradual movement toward allowing that awareness to exist without it needing to be resolved. This does not remove the sense of loss, or the awareness of what could not be, but it allows for something else to sit alongside it and life continues to move forward, shaped by what is now understood, even while carrying what cannot be changed.

Making Space for What Is Felt

When all of this becomes clear, there can be a lot to feel, and it comes in a plethora of emotions that do not arrive in a neat or manageable way. There can be grief for what was not recognised, anger at what was experienced, and a growing awareness of how much of life has been shaped by things that were never understood at the time.

There is also the reality of what continues because certain relationships are still, if not more difficult with new awareness. Environments are hard to navigate, and you become even more aware of the impact they have on you physically, expectations built around neurotypical ways of functioning are still present, and the effort required to deal with them does not go away. This is not something that can be neatly processed and then left behind, because it continues to be lived every moment of every day.

Trying to move past this phase or push it aside does not make it lessen and allowing the experiences to be there, even when they are uncomfortable or unresolved, becomes part of facing what is present rather than avoiding it. Making space for this is about allowing the full weight of what is felt to exist without minimising it, explaining it away, or turning it into something easier to carry.

There is no clear end point to this process, and the feelings may come and go, sometimes more intense, sometimes quieter, but they remain part of the wider experience. Allowing them does not stop life from continuing, but it does change the way it is lived, where what is real no longer must be pushed aside.

Not a Problem to Solve

There might be a strong pull to try and deal with grief in a way that makes it easier to carry, and for some this can take the form of spiritual bypassing, where spiritual language or ideas about meaning, purpose, or lessons are used to move past what is actually being felt. It can show up in beliefs that everything happens for a reason, or that there is something to learn that will make the experience acceptable, creating a sense that the feeling itself does not need to be fully faced.

For a while, this can seem to help, because it creates distance from the weight of what is there and so, experiences that are intense, confusing, or difficult to name can be reframed in a way that feels more manageable, particularly when there are no clear words to understand them psychologically. Physical sensations, shifts in awareness, and strong emotional responses may be interpreted as something significant or symbolic, rather than recognised as part of how the body and mind are responding to what has been lived.

As a clearer psychological understanding develops, that way of relating to these experiences often begins to change. What once needed to be explained through meaning or purpose becomes easier to accept, and the need to avoid hard truths gradually lessens as it becomes possible to stay with them as they are. The grief itself does not disappear, but the distance from it changes and instead of being explained away or reframed, it can be felt more directly, without needing to turn it into something else in order to cope.

In the context of a later autism diagnosis, this means allowing the grief for what was not understood, what was missed, and what cannot be changed to exist as it is, without trying to resolve it or reach a point where it no longer matters. There is no requirement to forgive in a way that removes the impact, and no expectation that it should become something that can be neatly completed before life continues.

Life moves forward with it rather than beyond it, and what begins to shift is not the presence of the feeling, but the way it is held, where acceptance comes from recognising what is there and allowing it to remain, rather than trying to change it into something easier to carry.

What Changes Through Recognition

As experiences are seen through a different lens, there may be a shift in how the past is understood and in how the self is now seen within it. What once felt like failure, confusion, or something personal begins to make more sense in a way that places it within a clearer understanding of why it happened.

This often brings a greater sense of self-compassion, along with a gradual softening of the way earlier experiences are judged. Actions and responses that were once criticised internally can begin to be seen in relation to the circumstances they developed within, where there was limited understanding, limited support, and often a need to cope without knowing what was being coped with. The expectation that things could have been handled differently begins to shift when it becomes clear that the awareness needed to do so was not available at the time.

In practical terms, this can change how certain experiences are remembered. Difficulties within relationships may no longer be understood as a lack of capacity, but as something shaped by not yet having the language or understanding to communicate needs, limits, or internal experiences. Situations that once felt like personal shortcomings can begin to make sense within environments that were not suited to the way the individual functioned, where expectations exceeded what was manageable and where there was little room for difference. It can also bring into view how often a person has been seen as too much in some situations and not enough in others, expected to adjust in ways that were never stable or sustainable. What was once held as evidence of not being enough can begin to be understood as a mismatch rather than a failure.

There can also be a change in how the opinions or interpretations of others are held. Where there was once a need to explain, justify, or be understood, there can be a clearer sense that personal limits exist for a reason, and that not all reactions from others need to be taken on or resolved. The absence of agreement does not carry the same weight when there is a stronger internal clarity about what is possible and what is not.

Alongside this, there can be a shift in how limits themselves are understood and what was once seen as not doing enough, or as letting others down, begins to be recognised in relation to what is manageable. Capacity is not endless, and it is not something that can be stretched indefinitely without consequence and so, what a person is able to give is closely tied to how regulated and stable their internal state is, and when that is overlooked, the cost is often paid in exhaustion, overwhelm, or withdrawal.

From this perspective, boundaries are no longer about being difficult or withholding, but about recognising the conditions under which it is possible to remain steady. Giving beyond that point does not create more connection or support, it often leads to dysregulation and a loss of the very capacity that was being relied upon. As this becomes clearer, the guilt that once accompanied limits can begin to lessen, replaced by a more grounded understanding of what is sustainable.

None of this removes the impact of what has been experienced, and it does not undo what has already taken place. What changes is the relationship to it, where there is less self-blame, less internal criticism, and a greater recognition of having done what was possible within the conditions that existed at the time.

From this place, there can be a different kind of steadiness, not because everything has been resolved, but because the need to see oneself as the problem begins to loosen, allowing for a more accurate and less critical understanding of what has been lived.

Continuing With Awareness

What has been seen cannot be erased, and there is no return to living in the same way as before. The past remains as it is, and the impact of what has been lived does not fade simply because it has been understood, yet the relationship to it begins to shift as that understanding settles.

Moving forward does not involve leaving any of it behind or reaching a point where it no longer matters but instead becomes a process of living alongside a clearer awareness of what was experienced, what was missed, and what is now known. That awareness starts to shape how situations are approached, how limits are recognised, and how meaning is made in the present, without needing to return to the same level of confusion or self-doubt that once surrounded those experiences.

There may still be moments where earlier patterns are felt or where the weight of what has been realised becomes more present again, particularly in situations that echo what has come before, yet these moments tend to be met differently when there is an understanding of what is happening and why. Rather than being pulled fully into those responses without clarity, there can be a growing ability to recognise them as they arise, creating a small but significant space between the experience and the response.

Within that space, there is more possibility for choice, even when that choice feels difficult or requires effort to hold. Limits can be recognised more quickly, and situations that once felt overwhelming or unclear can begin to make more sense in the moment, allowing for responses that are more aligned with what is needed.

Life continues in this way, not as a return to what was, and not as a complete separation from it, but as something that is lived with both past and present held in awareness. What has been recognised remains part of the picture, shaping what feels sustainable, what is possible, and what is no longer acceptable, while still allowing movement forward in a way that reflects that understanding.

Chapter Eleven: Advocacy Without Obligation

When Awareness Extends Beyond the Self

Attention also begins to reach externally, bringing a clearer view of how autism is viewed, misunderstood, and frequently overlooked in wider settings. What once felt like an isolated experience starts to become a shared experience, where similar patterns, responses, and difficulties can be recognised, not as identical experiences, but as something that shares a familiar shape.

This can change how everyday interactions are experienced and comments that once passed without much notice may begin to stand out as inaccurate or incomplete, with assumptions about behaviour or ability feeling increasingly misaligned with what is lived. There is a growing awareness of how often autistic experience is stereotyped, misrepresented, or missed entirely, and a sense of wanting to speak out and correct can emerge especially when witnessing others suffer the same unnecessary daily frustrations and challenges.

Noticing patterns in other people, where certain traits, struggles, or ways of responding begin to feel familiar is common in a way that was not previously understood. Although this does not come with the authority to define or diagnose, it can bring a quiet recognition, along with a sense that there is more present than is being acknowledged and feeling of wanting to help and support others in their early journey through assessment and diagnosis.

Holding this awareness can create a different kind of difficulty. The focus is no longer only on understanding oneself, but on navigating a wider environment where understanding is uneven, limited, or absent, and where what is now seen and acknowledged internally is not always reflected or recognised externally. In these moments, there can be a pull to respond, particularly when something important feels misunderstood or reduced, even when it is not always clear what that response should be.

When Speaking Out Meets Resistance

It becomes increasingly difficult to ignore how often autism is stereotyped and misunderstood, whether in everyday conversations, professional settings, or in passing remarks where lived experience is reduced to assumptions that do not reflect the reality of the autistic experience. What once might have gone unnoticed now stands out more clearly, not as isolated moments, but as part of a broader pattern in how individual autistic experience is interpreted and often misrepresented.

In these moments, there can be a pull to respond that goes beyond simply correcting and instead comes from a deeper need for things to be accurate, fair, and grounded in what is true. For many autistic people, this orientation towards clarity and correctness is not something that can be easily set aside, particularly when something is being misrepresented or reduced in a way that distorts the reality of lived experience, impacting everyday life. Saying something, then, is not about proving a point or winning an argument, but about bringing awareness and accuracy.

At the same time, speaking up does not ensure that what is said will be received in the way it is intended, and there can be little openness to questioning existing assumptions, particularly where doing so would require a shift in perspective or a recognition that something may have been viewed with limited and outdated understanding. Responses and insight may be dismissed, minimised, or met with defensiveness, allowing familiar narratives to remain intact without being openly discussed with curiosity.

This creates a particular kind of tension and frustration, where there is a growing clarity about what is inaccurate or missing, alongside an awareness that not every situation or individual will allow for that clarity to be recognised. Deciding when to speak, and when to step back, becomes part of navigating this as a way of recognising what is possible within a given interaction and what is a waste of time and energy.

There may be times where it feels necessary to address things, particularly where silence would mean allowing something harmful or misleading to go unchallenged, while at other times choosing not to engage reflects an understanding that the effort required is unlikely to lead to change or openness. Therefore, advocacy does not sit as a constant obligation, but takes shape in response to context, capacity, and a sense of what feels right in the moment for the individual.

Advocacy and the Weight of Responsibility

With this awareness comes a set of questions that are not easily resolved, particularly around what, if anything, should be done with what is now seen so clearly. Understanding how often autism is stereotyped and misunderstood brings attention to how much remains unchanged and how early research and diagnostic criteria is still based largely on white middle class autistic boys. As the research history has created such a narrow view of autism, it naturally raises the question of whether it becomes a personal mission to help challenge the stereotypes, and how far that responsibility should extend.

The answer is not straightforward because, in some moments, speaking up feels necessary, especially when something is inaccurate or dismissive, or when leaving it unchallenged would mean allowing harm or misunderstanding to continue. In other moments, the cost of doing so is more apparent, requiring time, energy, and emotional capacity that are not always available, and not always met with openness when offered.

This creates an ongoing tension between what feels fair and just and what feels personally sustainable. There is a pull towards contributing to change, towards helping others recognise themselves, or towards preventing the same misunderstandings from continuing, while also recognising that effort does not always lead to meaningful shifts. Attempts to raise awareness can be met with resistance or indifference, leaving a sense of having given more than was received, and at times adding to frustration although, occasionally, there are moments where something does land. A conversation may lead to curiosity and further questions, or someone may begin to recognise their own experience in a way that had not been possible before. These moments are often small, but they carry weight, particularly where they lead to greater awareness or access to support and this makes speaking out feel worthwhile.

Holding both realities makes it difficult to determine how much to give with the possibility of making a difference existing alongside the risk of becoming depleted. This brings the focus back to what is manageable on an individual level and in recognising what can be offered to the autistic community without impacting personal wellness.

The Cost of Constant Explanation

Choosing to speak out does not come without cost, particularly where what is offered is not received in a way that reflects the intention behind it. Repeated attempts to explain, clarify, or correct misunderstandings can begin to take a toll, especially when they are met with dismissal, minimisation, or a lack of willingness to engage more deeply with what is being said.

These responses may echo earlier experiences, where attempts to express difficulty or difference were overlooked, dismissed, or reduced, reinforcing a familiar pattern of not being fully heard or understood and when this repeats in adulthood, even in different settings, it can carry a similar weight in how it connects back to what has been experienced before.

In these moments, there can be a pull to keep explaining, to add more detail, more context, more reasoning, in the hope that clarity will lead to understanding, yet what often happens is that the more that is given, the less it is met, leaving the person in the position of trying to justify something that should not require justification. What begins as an attempt to be understood can shift into something far more draining, where the effort is no longer about communication, but about trying to make one's reality acceptable to someone who is not willing to recognise it.

When this happens, boundaries can begin to slip back without noticing, as the focus moves from simply stating what is true to trying to make it land, and when it does not, the instinct is to give more, explain further, and try again. The outcome often remains unchanged, and what is left is a sense of having to explain one's existence to people who have already decided not to receive it.

There is also a wider narrative that can shape these interactions, where expressions of difficulty are seen as unnecessary, exaggerated, or something that should simply be managed without discussion. In these environments, speaking openly about autistic experience can be met with impatience, dismissal, or the suggestion that it is something to "get on with," particularly where it challenges existing assumptions or requires any level of change or progression.

Engaging in this way becomes exhausting and requires emotional energy, clarity, and persistence, often without a corresponding sense of being met or understood, and when this pattern repeats, it can lead to a level of depletion that outweighs anything gained from continuing the conversation.

Because of this, any decision to advocate needs to take into consideration what is personally sustainable as living within environments that are not always accommodating already requires a significant level of adaptation, and adding the ongoing effort of explanation increases that load further. Finding a balance between speaking when it feels right and stepping back when it does not become part of maintaining that equilibrium.

Advocacy, where it is chosen, does not mean continuing to explain at the expense of oneself. It involves recognising when enough has been said, when boundaries need to be held, and when understanding is not something that can be created through further effort. And so, it becomes possible to engage without losing the steadiness that has already been hard won.

Advocacy in Different Forms

Advocacy does not need to take a single, visible form, and it does not always require a strong presence or a public voice to be meaningful. It can exist in quieter ways, shaped by what feels possible, appropriate, and sustainable for the individual, rather than by any expectation of how it should look.

For some, it may involve speaking openly in conversations where it feels relevant, naming autism and sharing experience in a way that brings understanding into spaces where it might otherwise be absent. This can happen informally, in social settings, in classes, or in interactions with professionals, where a moment arises and something is said that would not have been said before. At times, these conversations can also lead to something more, where another person begins to recognise aspects of their own experience and considers the possibility of autism in a way they had not before, sometimes taking steps to explore this further with professionals.

At other times, it may take a more deliberate form, such as raising concerns, offering feedback, or suggesting changes where something is inaccessible or inappropriate. This might involve sending an email, challenging a policy, or pointing out where adjustments could be made, even where that input is not always received or acted upon.

It can also be expressed through choice, in the environments that are entered or avoided, and in the decisions made about what to engage with and what to step away from. Choosing not to return to a place that refuses to accommodate, not to support a service that does not consider accessibility, or not to participate in something that feels fundamentally misaligned are all forms of communication, even when nothing is said directly.

And so, advocacy is not limited to speaking out, but is also present in what is withdrawn, declined, or no longer tolerated. It can be reflected in how life is organised around what is manageable, in the boundaries that are held, and in the refusal to continue adapting to environments that do not offer the same consideration in return.

There are also forms of advocacy that extend outward more gradually, through writing, sharing experiences, contributing ideas, or offering perspective where it may be useful, which all contribute to a broader shift in understanding. Taken together, these different forms reflect a way of engaging that does not just rely on heavy visibility or volume, but on alignment, choice, and a clear sense of what feels right, while also recognising that advocacy is not a requirement, and that choosing not to engage in it at all is equally valid.

When Silence Is Not Absence

Choosing not to engage at all is also valid and reflects something far more deliberate, where a decision is made to protect energy, maintain a regulated nervous system, and prioritise personal well-being in a way that has not always been possible before.

For many autistic people, this shift carries particular significance, especially where much of life has involved placing others first, meeting expectations that override internal signals, or adapting to environments that do not recognise or accommodate difference. Where early experiences may have involved having needs minimised, overlooked, or shaped by the limitations of others, learning to step back can represent a fundamental change in how those needs are understood and protected.

And so, choosing not to engage is a form of self-preservation that is sometimes necessary. It reflects an awareness of what continued engagement can cost, particularly where understanding is unlikely to be met, and where the effort required would come at the expense of a calmer, more grounded internal state that has taken time to build.

There is a difference between not speaking and having nothing to say and silence, in this sense, can hold clarity, discernment, and a recognition of limits that were not always acknowledged before. While this distinction may not be recognised externally, it can become increasingly clear internally, where the decision to step back is guided by what supports regulation, rather than what meets expectation.

Placed within the wider context of late recognition, unmet needs, and the ongoing effort of navigating environments that do not always accommodate autistic experience, prioritising oneself is not excessive or unnecessary. It is a necessary rebalancing, where what has been consistently overridden begins to take precedence.

Navigating Misunderstanding

Greater awareness does not prevent misunderstandings and even where there is clarity, self understanding, and a more grounded way of responding, interactions may still be shaped by assumptions that do not reflect what is being expressed. For many autistic people, particularly those who value accuracy, fairness, and being understood as intended, this can remain uncomfortable.

What changes is how it is responded to and misunderstanding no longer becomes something that must be chased, corrected, or taken on as a personal responsibility. There may be less inclination to keep adjusting, explaining, or softening what is being said in the hope that it will be received differently, and less willingness to override what is known internally to maintain ease or connection.

This can become more visible in moments that would once have been handled differently. For example, noticing that something does not sit right in the body when another person behaves in a way that feels off, and choosing to speak to it directly rather than holding it in, redirecting it elsewhere, or minimising its significance. What is expressed is not intended to judge or correct, but to remain aligned with what is being felt within even if the way it is received may be misunderstood, dismissed, or met with defensiveness.

Where this would once have required further effort to repair, explain, or manage, there can instead be a clearer boundary around what belongs to whom. The response of the other person remains with them, including how they interpret, feel, or react and what remains with oneself is the recognition of what was felt within and the decision to express it.

This reflects a significant shift from earlier patterns where the emotions and reactions of others may have needed to be anticipated, absorbed, or managed, particularly in dynamics where this was expected. When this has been a longstanding way of relating, there can be a tendency to associate connection with keeping others comfortable, even where this comes at a personal cost. Allowing others to hold their own responses without taking them on board as something to fix begins to change that dynamic. The result is a feeling of doing the right thing for oneself, being authentic and remaining true to personal values and morals without overriding them to allow others to stay comfortable.

This change in self-trust, responses and expression can lead to a different kind of connection, where some people are able to meet what is expressed with openness and discussion, while others may not.

Those who are willing to engage with honesty and reflection are more likely to remain, while those who are uncomfortable with it may fall away. What remains is shaped less by how something is received, and more by the ability to remain aligned with oneself, resulting in increased self-trusr and better relationship dynamics.

Continuing Without Pressure

When advocacy is not driven by obligation but choice, there is less need to represent, explain, or justify, and more space to engage when it feels possible, and to step back when it does not.

This shift is not limited to the experience of autism and extends into wider experiences, such as the experience of enmeshment and parentification mentioned in this book, that may not have been recognised previously. As awareness develops, so does the ability to see more clearly what is and is not yours to hold and from there, the focus changes. It is no longer about proving something to others, or taking responsibility for how something is received, but about remaining aligned with yourself, guided by self awareness, self-ordained boundaries, autonomy, and developed self-trust.

This does not remove challenge and there may still be moments where something difficult needs to be addressed and when discomfort in doing so is part of growth. But the difference is that it no longer involves overriding yourself to meet expectations, or allowing yourself to be pushed, minimised, or drawn into questioning what is already felt and known within.

From there, it no longer sits as something that needs to be maintained or performed, but as something that is engaged with when it feels aligned and right for the individual; without the pull to explain, justify, or ensure you have been understood. Other people's responses are no longer something that needs to be managed, and there is stringer conviction to remain with what feels true to oneself whether it is met with acceptance or not.

Chapter Twelve: Integration in Practice

No Final State

There is no final place to arrive at where everything becomes resolved, understood, or easy, and the life patterns experienced and described throughout this book do not simply disappear or change. The environments and dynamics that shaped them often remain much the same, along with the people, expectations, and limitations that were always present.

What changes is how these are recognised and responded to and situations that once created confusion or self-doubt may begin to feel more familiar, not because they have improved, but because there is a clearer understanding of what is happening and why. The external experience may look very similar, yet internally it no longer holds the same weight or authority, and you are able to see through it in order to change your own responses.

There are still moments where things feel overwhelming and challenging, even more so at times, where old responses are triggered, or where the impact of others and the wider environment is felt in ways that cannot always be avoided. What begins to shift is the meaning attached to those moments, where they are no longer taken as evidence of any personal failure, or as something that must be fixed to move forward.

Instead, there is a gradual sense of being able to remain with what is happening without losing connection to oneself. What once led to disorientation or a need to adapt beyond what was sustainable can be recognised more quickly, and held with greater clarity, even when the situation itself has not changed.

Living With Greater Alignment

Living with greater alignment is not a final place that is reached and then maintained, but something that continually develops and adjusts through experience, reflection, and the gradual recognition of what does and does not feel true to oneself. It is shaped personally rather than defined externally, and as circumstances shift and understanding deepens.

For an autistic person, this can begin to look like a quiet movement away from adapting to neurotypical expectations as a default and towards responding in ways that are more closely guided by the autistic experience. What this often brings into focus is the extent to which life has been shaped by masking, by learning to adjust, and present in ways that are acceptable to others, even where this comes at a personal cost. That cost may not always have been fully visible at the time, particularly where it was necessary for connection, safety, or belonging, yet it can become harder to ignore once it has been fully recognised.

As this awareness develops, what once felt required may begin to feel unsustainable, and in some cases, impossible to continue in the same way. The effort involved in maintaining a version of oneself that meets expectation, while remaining disconnected from what is felt within, can create a tension that is difficult to hold indefinitely. Alignment, in this sense, is not about becoming something new, but about no longer being able to maintain what was never fully true.

This does not unfold in a straightforward way. Familiar patterns can still appear, and there may be moments where external pressures pull responses back towards what has always been done, particularly where those patterns were formed over long periods of time. What begins to shift within this is the awareness of it, where something that might previously have gone unnoticed is recognised in the moment or shortly after, allowing a different response to become possible, even if only in small ways at first.

Alongside this, there is often a growing clarity around what belongs to oneself and what has been taken on from others, whether that is expectation, belief, or emotional responsibility. As that distinction becomes more visible, decisions can begin to move away from imitation or obligation and towards what is manageable, creating a way of living that is shaped less by what is expected and more by what is known internally.

This remains an ongoing, lifelong way of living rather than a set outcome, often confusing and at times unclear, where movement is guided more by awareness than by certainty. But what matters is not arriving at a finished version of alignment but continuing to relate to what is felt as right internally in the moment, even when personal morals, values and boundaries are still developing.

What Changes, and What Does Not

As alignment begins to take shape, there can be a gradual shift in how life is experienced, not because everything around a person changes, but because what is seen with new awareness leads to a clearer sense of limits, a better understanding of what is manageable, and a growing willingness to respond to internal signals rather than override them to meet expectation.

As this clarity develops, what no longer feels aligned becomes harder to ignore. Roles that once felt normal may begin to show themselves and feel unhealthy, relationships that were sustained through adaptation can start to feel one-sided, and environments that relied on a previous version of oneself may no longer feel workable in the same way.

There may also be a period where things feel less settled, and there is high anxiety around putting boundaries in place and the reactions it receives, where the old and familiar no longer fits, yet what is emerging has not fully taken its shape. This can bring a sense of being in between, where there is less external stability even though there is more internal awareness.

At the same time, much of the wider environment remains unchanged and continues in the same way. The world still feels overwhelming, too noisy and confusing, misunderstandings can still occur, and there may continue to be situations that require a certain level of adjustment because these realities are not removed through awareness, nor are they resolved through better understanding alone.

What does change is the relationship to these experiences, where there is less inclination to adapt at any cost, further awareness and acceptance of personal limits, and more recognition of when something is not workable, even if that creates difficulty for others. Alignment does not necessarily bring ease, but it allows for a way of living that is less divided, where what is maintained externally no longer comes at the same internal cost as it once was.

Moving Forward in Awareness and Alignment

There may still be many unanswered questions, parts of the past may remain unresolved, and some experiences do not make sense in a way that feels complete or satisfying, yet life does not wait for everything to be resolved, and it moves on regardless. What becomes possible instead is a different kind of acceptance, one that allows movement forward without needing everything to be fully explained or resolved and this brings a sense of inner peace and freedom that has not been experienced before. There is less internal battle, less trying to change others to feel at peace and more self-awareness and trust.

There may still be moments of uncertainty, and there may still be challenge, but less energy is spent maintaining a version of the self that does not fit and instead, one checks in with oneself and asks Does this feel right for me? Am I okay with this? Is this what I desire? Does this align with my values and morals?

These changes can bring grief for what was not seen or expressed earlier, for what may have been different with earlier self-awareness, understanding or support that was not available at the time, and for the length of time spent adapting in ways that came at a cost. That grief does not go away, but it no longer needs to be pushed aside or avoided away to continue living a fulfilled life, and you no longer feel guilty for having negative feelings about those who let you down, when at the same time you recognise that they were also limited in their awareness.

Externally, much may remain the same within family dynamics, friendships, relationships and work settings. Environments may still be overwhelming and overstimulating, misunderstandings still occur, and there may continue to be limits that require some level of adjustment or distance. Living in a society that has not been built with autistic experiences in mind continue to require navigation, but what changes is how these realities are met. There is more clarity around what belongs to you and what does not, and a more accurate sense of what is manageable without tipping into overwhelm. A stronger sense of self-trust develops as something that can be returned to at any time and although insight from others may still be valuable it no longer replaces inner truth and decisions that feel best for you.

These changes do not make things easier in the short term and in many ways, it can feel more difficult. However, it is more authentic and ultimately results in a fuller, more peaceful existence guided from within. Relationships may change or fall away, familiar dynamics may no longer hold, and there can be periods of distance or uncertainty where what once felt established no longer fits but there is something more honest within that.

What remains at this point is not a perfected life, but a more conscious and self-guided one. The same person remains, but with a clearer sense of where they end and others begin, and from here, there is simply a different way of living.

Chapter Thirteen: Epilogue: Coming Home to Yourself

If there is one thing I hope this book leaves you with, it is the understanding that there was never anything broken or wrong with being your authentic self.

Many autistic people spend years trying to understand why life feels more difficult than it appears to be for those around them. In the absence of answers, it is easy to become focused on what feels difficult, what seems different, and what does not fit comfortably within the expectations of the world around us.

Receiving an autism diagnosis does not change the past. It does not erase difficult experiences or provide answers to every question. What it can offer is a different perspective; one that allows us to view ourselves with greater clarity, compassion, and understanding. Experiences that once felt confusing may begin to make more sense. Shame may begin to loosen its grip. There can be relief in realising that many of the struggles we carried were never personal failings at all.

Throughout this book, I have explored themes of adaptation, masking, identity, parentification, relationships, self-trust, and authenticity. Although these experiences may look different from one person to the next, they often share a common thread: the gradual process of getting to know ourselves beneath everything that taught us who we were supposed to be.

For some, this may involve recognising that they were never responsible for carrying the emotional weight of other people's lives. For others, it may involve questioning long-held beliefs about who they are, or beginning to take their own thoughts, feelings, needs, and experiences more seriously.

Coming home to yourself is not about becoming someone new. Rather, it is the process of returning to what was always there beneath conditioning, societal expectations, and the roles we learned to occupy. The parts that had to hide were not weaknesses; they were parts of you that learned to adapt to survive.

The work of getting to know ourselves is not about becoming someone new. It is about recognising and reclaiming the parts of ourselves that were pushed aside, hidden, or forgotten along the way.

Perhaps coming home to yourself is not about finding something that was missing but remembering what was there all along and perhaps now those parts can begin to come home.

www.ingramcontent.com/pod-product-compliance
Lightning Source LLC
LaVergne TN
LVHW050934210926
848482LV00013B/610
9781068753336